LIVING AND DYING
WITH CONFIDENCE

LIVING
AND DYING
WITH
CONFIDENCE

A DAY-BY-DAY GUIDE

ANYEN RINPOCHE
& Allison Choying Zangmo

FOREWORD BY KATHLEEN DOWLING SINGH

Wisdom

Wisdom Publications
199 Elm Street
Somerville, MA 02144 USA
wisdompubs.org

Library of Congress Cataloging-in-Publication Data
Names: Anyen, Rinpoche, author. | Zangmo, Allison Choying, author. | Singh,
    Kathleen Dowling, writer of foreword.
Title: Living and dying with confidence : a day-by-day guide by Anyen
    Rinpoche & Allison Choying Zangmo ; foreword by Kathleen Dowling Singh.
Description: Somerville, MA : Wisdom Publications, 2016. | Includes index.
Identifiers: LCCN 2015041227 (print) | LCCN 2015041728 (ebook) | ISBN
    9781614292289 (pbk. : alk. paper) | ISBN 1614292280 (pbk. : alk. paper) |
    ISBN 9781614292432 (ebook) | ISBN 1614292434 (ebook)
Subjects: LCSH: Death—Religious aspects—Buddhism. | Death—Planning.
Classification: LCC BQ4487 .A595 2016 (print) | LCC BQ4487 (ebook) | DDC
    202/.3—dc23
LC record available at http://lccn.loc.gov/2015041227

ISBN 978-1-61429-228-9   ebook ISBN 978-1-61429-243-2

20 19 18 17 16   5 4 3 2 1

Cover design by Phil Pascuzzo.
Interior design by Gopa & Ted2, Inc. Set in ITC Galliard Pro 10.125/14.7.

Wisdom Publications' books are printed on acid-free paper and meet
the guidelines for permanence and durability of the Production
Guidelines for Book Longevity of the Council on Library Resources.

❀ This book was produced with environmental mindfulness.
For more information, please visit wisdompubs.org/wisdom-environment.

Printed in the United States of America.

Please visit fscus.org.

Dedication

For our root lama, Tsara Dharmakirti Rinpoche, who attained the fearless stronghold of death and passed away while resting in the dharmakaya; for Dorlo Rinpoche whose accomplishment equaled the span of his life; and for all of the lineage masters who have given their lives to maintain the stainless purity of the teachings for the benefit of all sentient beings.

Table of Contents

Foreword

AT THE VERY HEART of each of us is a longing for the sacred. We have an innate intuition that there is more to life than only self and mere appearance; we have a yearning to know that deeper reality and live within it. This is so now and it has been so for millennia.

Throughout time, many have stepped into that deep pull of longing, surrendering to its call. Our wisdom traditions are the rich legacy of their spiritual explorations. The realizations gained through their longing and inquiry transformed their minds and their experience of being. They awakened into fulfillment, just as we long to do. But although they may have wished to pass their realizations along—simply hand them over to us—realization, inner knowing, is not a secondhand but a first-hand experience.

The saints, sages, yogis, and holy beings taught all that was teachable, shared all that could be shared. Within various wisdom lineages, they invited others into their wordless, invisible transformations by sharing their aerial view—the testimony of their realizations. Unable to transfer their realizations or the transformations grace effected in them, they shared accounts of the practices they engaged in, taught the steps they followed to recognize grace and end all perceived and conceived separation from it.

They taught *Dharma*. *Dharma* is a word that transcends lineages. Its meaning holds a sense both of "the truth" and "the path that leads to the truth." It encompasses all that can be taught in response to our deep spiritual yearning: wisdom, and the practices that allow us to arrive at wisdom.

Through the centuries, hundreds of thousands of longing souls followed these great spiritual explorers. Inspired by the views that pointed toward that deeper reality, they took up the practices of the lineages to which they had geographical access. These practices were taught and engaged primarily in secluded communities—in monasteries, abbeys, and convents, in caves, forests, and deserts.

Now, in our time, we have access to many noble traditions, all gloriously available to us. In these last decades—the age of information—the river of Dharma is not only transcending geographic borders, it's transcending the monastery. In response to contemporary longing, *Dharma* has poured out from behind the cloister walls, and the waters of that beautiful river are irrigating the fields where we live.

For ages, it was widely held that awakening was only possible for those with a monastic lifestyle. With Dharma now flowing far and wide, the way has opened for awakening to be a reasonable expectation for sincere lay practitioners as well. The intentions and the practices are the same; they lead us all to the grace for which we've longed.

In this book, the revered teacher Anyen Rinpoche and his student Allison Choying Zangmo offer Tibetan Buddhist monastic wisdom, accumulated and refined over more than a thousand years in meditation halls high in the Himalayas. They share the views and time-honored practices of the traditional Tibetan stages of the path to enlightenment.

Speaking to our common longing, Rinpoche and Allison present a clear and structured year-long guide of meditations and contemplations. Through thoughtful questions based on these deliberately sequential contemplations, they ask us to explore our own minds, to open to our struggles and impermanence. They suggest exercises throughout the day so that we can practice authentically in the midst of our busy lives—just as we are living them.

Moral discipline based on mind training and an understanding of karma, renunciation that sees the suffering nature of ordinary mind, and *bodhichitta*—a heart filled with wisdom and compassion—are called forth and cultivated in us as the stages of the path are followed. An openness to living and a fearlessness in any circumstance, including death, become possible when we rest in awakened awareness, beyond self-reference.

A year spent with this book as guide can assist practitioners from any tradition in the holy tasks of emptying the mind and opening the heart. *Living and Dying with Confidence* is a great kindness, making available to all of us a view of compassionate wisdom and the steps to making that view our own realized awareness—in our living and in our dying.

Kathleen Dowling Singh

Introduction

REFLECTING ON DEATH and its elusive, mysterious nature is a fundamental part of many spiritual traditions. The Tibetan Buddhist tradition, in particular, places a special emphasis on the moment of death as being laden with potential for spiritual awakening and the transcendence of ordinary mind. Tibetans describe the moment of death as a time where the mind is "imprinted"—either by fearless love and compassion, or by strong emotions such as fear, regret, and doubt. For that reason, the yogis of Tibet spend their lives attempting to surpass ordinary fears, so that when they suddenly see the face of death, they can fearlessly rely upon their spiritual training and die in perfectly relaxed, mindful meditative equipoise.

From this came a great many of the traditional practices in the Tibetan Buddhist tradition, especially the one called *chod*, or "cutting through attachment to the body." Traditionally, this practice is performed by extremely realized yogis, or *chodpas*, who inhabit the charnel grounds. Based on special training, these chodpas bless the bodies of the dead according to tradition and then cut and offer the bodies of the deceased to vultures. This tradition of offering a corpse as spiritual nourishment is called a "sky burial." A sky burial has spiritual benefit for all of the beings involved: first, it enables the yogi to face the fear of death; second, it benefits the deceased, whose body is both blessed and offered as sustenance to another being; and finally, it benefits the vultures, who receive blessings and sustenance from the yogi. Anyen Rinpoche's uncle,

Lama Dampal, was such a chodpa. Rinpoche said that his uncle's mastery was such that when he used mantras to call the vultures to the charnel ground, the proper number always came; the birds never had to fight among themselves for food. The entire practice is infused with fearless blessings and love.

Our modern American lives are tame in many ways in comparison to the esoteric yogic traditions of Tibet. However, while we may not be able to inhabit charnel grounds and bless the bodies of the deceased as a way to transcend our fears of mortality, we can still challenge ourselves to let go of the attachment we have to this life, and the fears we have of dying. This twelve-month training program challenges us to face the many layers of fear and denial we have developed, personally and as a culture, in our wish to avoid the certainty of death. The daily reflections and tasks included in this book were designed to invoke discomfort—to show us where we are vulnerable and how far we have to go in order to face our own mortality and that of those we love.

This book is meant to be both practical and interactive. Each day, it gives a specific idea to contemplate, questions to reflect on, and a task to perform. Choose a time each day to read the entry for that day, and spend a little time contemplating and completing the suggested task. Many of the entries ask you to list ideas or qualities, or to describe your thoughts on a certain topic. Please use a dedicated journal to keep track of these entries.

While it is not necessary to start on any particular day of the year, we do encourage you to keep with the training program for the entire year, without doubling up or skipping ahead. Also, you may find that some of the contemplations, especially those included in the first month, are difficult to reflect on. Remember that these exercises were designed to help each of us see the strong attachments we have to our bodies, our lives, our loved ones, and our material possessions. As a result, painful emotions such as fear and anxiety are bound to arise. If this occurs, take a few moments to breathe deeply and reflect on the impermanent nature of your thoughts and emotions before continuing. At the end of the year, you will have an excellent tool to help you examine your own strengths and weaknesses, see your growth over the year, and also see how far you have yet to go.

Because of the difficult nature of this program, we envisioned readers using this book with a sangha or a small group: a web of spiritual practitioners who can mutually support each other through the process of preparing for death, and for the actual process of death itself. Even if you don't live near your spiritual brothers and sisters, you can make use of technology to offer each other mutual support throughout the year.

We hope that those of you who have already read *Dying with Confidence* will use this book to take your work even further. For those readers who are not familiar with the Dying with Confidence training program and the Phowa Foundation, we hope that this book can serve as an introduction to Anyen Rinpoche's vision and a great tool on your spiritual path.

May all sentient beings achieve a fearless, compassionate state of mind at the moment of death!

Anyen Rinpoche
Allison Choying Zangmo

As your first entry in your journal, please take a few moments to write down your goals for this year of contemplative training, and also make some notes on what your current daily spiritual practice consists of, if you have one.

Waking Up to the Reality of Death

M OST OF THE TIME we believe that our lives consist of a closed system. We understand and identify all of the possibilities that could be encountered on a daily basis. Because we think we know all that there is to know, we progress through life unaware of all of the difficult and painful things that are bound to happen. No wonder that when we see or hear about another's emotional suffering, illness, or even death, our first instinct is to push it away. Some of us even go so far as to avoid reading the newspaper or watching the television in order to avoid hearing about the suffering experienced by others. We say things like, "I just want to focus on the good things in my own life." In other words, we want to keep ourselves insulated and isolated within the closed system we have built.

Having to make an emotional connection with the reality of death throws our whole belief system out of whack. After all, when we designed our version of the world, we did not make allowances for the unknown. We failed to plan for the reality of death. But if we examine more deeply, we find that the problem is not the existence of suffering in the world; the problem is the closed system itself. In a closed system, emotional stability relies on compartmentalizing: shutting out and excluding unpleasant and unwanted experiences and avoiding the very reality we live in.

This may serve us for a time. But what happens when our spouse, our parents, our children get sick and pass away right before our eyes?

What about when we get sick and we're forced to look death straight in the eye?

On the Mahayana Buddhist path, we commit to following the way of a bodhisattva—a compassionate hero or heroine. The very first question we must face when we step on the bodhisattva path is this: This closed system we spend so much time building—*are we brave enough to let it collapse?*

Day 1

Depending on our upbringing, culture, and personality, we might have very different ideas concerning death. Some of us were raised with a specific set of religious beliefs, such as being reborn in heaven and experiencing everlasting life, and some of us were taught just the opposite—that life and consciousness cease at the moment of death. For others of us, death was never even something that we talked about with our families.

But whatever our beliefs are, we can be sure that they will color our experience during this year-long contemplation on death and dying. It is important we take some time to reflect on what we actually believe will happen when we die, so that we know where we're starting from and we're cognizant of our spiritual journey over the next year of exploration.

Take a few minutes to journal today about your thoughts and beliefs about the experience of death. Of the ideas you grew up with, which have you held on to? Which have you discarded? Don't judge your ideas or worry if they seem contradictory or are not well formed. At the end of the year, you can look back at this entry to see how your thoughts and convictions have changed.

DAY 2

All of us have experienced death. Even if we haven't yet experienced the loss of someone close, we've all been touched by another's death. For example, we may be affected by the passing of an influential or inspirational leader. Although so many years have passed since the assassinations of Martin Luther King Jr. and John F. Kennedy, many of us can still remember exactly what we were doing the moment that our nation began to mourn its losses. Others of us are too young to have personally experienced the passing of these great leaders, but probably all of us remember when the nation grieved the events of September 11, 2001.

What has been your personal experience of death thus far? Have you experienced the loss of someone close, such as a parent, a sibling, or even a pet? What was that experience like? Try to find words that characterize your particular thoughts and emotions from that time.

DAY 3

In order to get ahead and get what we want for ourselves, we're driven to work hard and succeed in our careers. We have very little time to enjoy ourselves. Some of us may only have a few weeks of holiday each year. When we have time off, we may not want to spend it visiting an elderly family member or a loved one who is ill. As our grandparents and parents get older, we may not see them often because they may live in another city, state, or even another country.

In other parts of the world, many children take care of their parents when they get older, but in America, not many of us have the time. And to be fair, many parents do not wish to give up their independence and be cared for by children they raised themselves. Parents, as well as their children, do not like to acknowledge aging, illness, or death. As a result, death is hidden from many of us. It's not that we are actively avoiding death as much as death just doesn't fit into our lifestyle, our beliefs, or our society. But at what cost?

☞ Reflect on how we, as well as others around us, feel lonely, disconnected, and fearful. Think about how these feelings affect our attitudes toward death.

Day 4

How do we avoid thinking about death? One habit many of us have is to keep ourselves incredibly busy. We wake up early, go to the office, focus on the task at hand, surf the web on our laptop or cellphone when we have a free moment, finish work, stop at the bank or the store on the way home, and arrive home in the evening too exhausted to think about anything. Once home, we still need to look after our spouses, children, and pets, as well as make sure we have paid the bills and fulfilled all of our other obligations.

But what happens when we face something that slows us down? For example, an illness invades our own body, or a loved one's, or a friend or family member suddenly dies. How will we cope when our closed system suddenly tears open?

☞ Today, take a look at how you organize your time. Do you make yourself so busy that you have no time to connect, feel, or reflect?

Day 5

Relationships are another mechanism we have built into our lives to help us avoid the certainty of death. In much the same way that we keep ourselves busy and exhausted by working, we can also busy ourselves by entering into a complicated relationship that strips us of the mental and emotional energy that might lead us to question the true nature of our fleeting lives.

We often feel consumed by relationships or enter into unhealthy relationships that we know aren't good for us. Although this can leave us feeling depleted, at the same time there may be a sense of comfort in how the relationship helps us shut down. We do not have to examine our lives any deeper. The relationship fits neatly into the model of our closed system, and even reinforces it.

▰▷ Today, take some time to reflect on relationships. How are your relationships spiritually nurturing? In what ways do they encourage you to shut down?

Day 6

How else do we keep ourselves shut down—too exhausted to question how we live, too closed off to see the pain and suffering of others, too hardened to engage in meaningful spiritual practice? Anything in our daily lives can become an addiction that helps to maintain our closed system: work, food, sex, drugs, alcohol, computer gaming, social media, television, emotional drama. We should begin to identify the ways in which we distract ourselves from what is going on in our lives.

Real life is far different from the fantasy we concoct in our minds. It is full of pain and suffering. It is full of uncertainty and change. It is full of unpleasant experiences, and things that are out of our control. The specifics of our death are the paramount uncertainty. It is symbolic of all of the things we wish to avoid.

▰▷ How do you keep yourself distracted and shut down, unaware of life's momentary nature?

DAY 7

We tend to think that bad things happen to others, and not to us. On some deeper level, we believe we are the exception. For example, when we hear about someone else developing cancer or a terminal illness, it can seem unreal and distant from our own experience. When we hear about the death of another, we may feel sad and even grieve, but much of the time we fail to make a personal connection to what is happening. Feeling saddened by bad news is one thing. It is quite another thing to understand that in just the same way others become ill, get old, and die, so our own lives will pass.

We live in a deeply logical society. We are trained to look for patterns and connections. Yet for some reason, we struggle to apply what we see happening in the rest of the world to ourselves. We grasp on to the idea that we are somehow unique and different. We fail to understand our own mortality.

✎▷ What fantasies about being unique and exceptional do you have that enable you to avoid contemplating the inevitability of your own death?

DAY 8

We complement avoiding the reality of death with fantasies of immortality. We may not believe in heaven or immortal life, but there are many ways that we fantasize about stopping the passage of time. We may work hard to achieve something great, so our name will go down in history and will not be forgotten. We may have children to carry on our family name and keep a piece of us in this world. We may spend thousands of dollars on skin creams or plastic surgery to resist aging. We may buy clothes that we would have worn in our twenties, or date someone many years our junior. All of these reflect our intrinsic denial of the reality of our own deaths.

How are you perpetuating the belief that your life will go on continuously? How can you fully acknowledge that the passing of each day brings you closer to death?

DAY 9

There has never been a person who was born who did not, or will not, die. Even if we call to mind the most powerful leaders, wealthiest businessmen, or most intelligent scientists, none of them had the means to transcend death. Even with all of the advances of modern medicine and technology, people may live longer, but they eventually have to die.

The life of the Buddha is an example of the reality of death. Although Buddha Shakyamuni attained complete enlightenment during his lifetime, he was born into an ordinary human body, and so he died an ordinary, human death as he attained the state of parinirvana. It is said that the Buddha did not want to inspire the fantasy that even spiritual mastery could enable one to evade death.

Today, reflect on how death is the shared fate of all living beings.

DAY 10

Today, do some research on demographics. How many people take birth each minute around the world? How many people die each minute, each day, each year? Notice that mortality rates are higher in certain areas of the world. Are you surprised to find out that more than 150,000 people die around the planet each day?

Day 11

You may be surprised to learn that in early human history, average life expectancy was only ten years—radically skewed by an extremely high infant mortality rate. Moreover, some estimate that more than 100 billion people have died from ancient times until now.

In our modern world, it is much easier to have the illusion that life will continue on and that death is unnatural because of the low infant mortality rate in the United States and the fact that many of us live long, healthy lives. However, even this does not change the inevitability of death.

✏️ Today, try to fathom how many people have ever lived on the Earth.

Day 12

Each person who dies has their own story, just like we do. Like us, their lives are filled with things they do not want to leave behind—spouse, children, extended family members, friends, their home, wealth, and possessions.

In the Buddhist teachings, we call birth, aging, sickness, and death the "four great rivers." From the point of view of being carried by these four great rivers, all human beings are fundamentally the same. There is not even one of us who is going to avoid the pain and suffering of human life, and not one of us will cheat death in the end.

✏️ Today, reflect on the forces that carry us, as well as all other beings, through life: birth, aging, sickness, and death.

Day 13

Death will come to us, just as it comes to others around us.

▰⇒ Today, find a newspaper or online source and read the obituary section. Notice how the people described there are of all ages and of many different backgrounds. Try to notice any specific details in the obituaries that help you connect with the humanity of a person who died. Did they leave behind a spouse or children? Did they live in a town or a neighborhood similar to your own? Try to imagine details of the deceased person's life and feel a shared connection with them.

Day 14

Death will come to us, just as it has come to everyone who has come before us. Is a cemetery located in your city or town? Chances are there is more than one, since there is no shortage of people who die and need to be buried.

▰⇒ Find a cemetery, and take a walk through the gravestones on your lunch hour or after work. Notice how many people are buried there. Take some time to look at the headstones. Notice the years in which people were born and when they died. Notice how old each person was. Each gravestone was paid for and designed by a loving family member or relative. However, even the loving relatives of the deceased may no longer be alive. Today, try to connect with the reality of death for some of the deceased and their family members, understanding that you share this same reality.

DAY 15

Death is around us at every moment. In the Buddhist teachings, death is described as a lord who beckons us when our time is up, but if we pay attention we'll see that death is nearby at every moment.

▰▷ Today, notice all of the examples of death that you encounter during your day. Notice a dead fly on the windowsill; leaves falling from the trees; an old, abandoned house; fruit that has fallen from a tree and begun to rot; the end of a relationship; a vase of flowers that need to be thrown out; a car accident on the highway; an ambulance run. Where else do you find death today?

DAY 16

We cannot know when or how death will come to us or to anyone else.

▰▷ Today, notice an older person. While looking at them, imagine how long they may have to live. Then, notice a baby, a toddler, or a young child, and imagine how long they may have to live. Observe your own preconceived ideas about when death should come. Notice how unjust it feels that the elderly person could outlive the child.

DAY 17

There once was a woman named Kisa Gotami, the wife of a rich businessman, whose infant son fell ill and died. Kisa Gotami was overwhelmed by grief and could not accept the death of her child. She carried the baby around her village asking if there was anyone who had medicine that could heal him. One kind person said, "I know of a great physician," and sent her to see Buddha Shakyamuni.

Kisa Gotami took her child before Buddha Shakyamuni and requested that the Buddha give him medicine that would heal him from illness. The Buddha said, "I will give you the medicine you request, but first you must bring to me a mustard seed from the home of a family where no one has lost a loved one."

Kisa Gotami was eager for her son to be healed, so she went from door to door asking for a mustard seed. At first, no one refused her request. They were happy to give a seed to heal a sick child. However, before taking the mustard seed she said, "I must receive the mustard seed from a home where no family member or loved one has died." And then no one was able to give it to her.

After some time, Kisa Gotami realized what the Buddha was trying to tell her. She came to understand that death is a part of life, and there is no person unaffected by the experience of death. She buried her child and gave up worldly life altogether, becoming a student of the Buddha and eventually attaining a highly realized state.

Today, consider that every person you have ever met has been affected by death. What are the implications of this?

DAY 18

We should cultivate a heart and mind that is capable of connecting deeply with all sentient beings. Although this may start as an ordinary feeling of connection, ultimately it becomes what we call *bodhichitta*, or the mind of enlightenment. When we cultivate bodhichitta, we are willing to tie our own circumstances to another's without considering the personal cost or the difficulty it may bring us. Not only are we willing to be open to the suffering of others, we are also willing to dedicate our efforts to their own happiness and well-being.

If we fear the experiences of suffering and death, both our own and another's, how can we truly be open, loving, and compassionate toward others? Awakening to the reality of death is not only about overcoming our personal fears. It is also about removing the barriers to connecting with others. It is about being willing to be inconvenienced, vulnerable, and in a constant state of flux as we work with changing circumstances.

▰▷ Today, reflect on what it might mean for you yourself to live more open to others, more vulnerably.

DAY 19

A person who commits to the Buddhist path is called a *bodhisattva*: a compassionate hero or heroine. Against all odds, a bodhisattva has found the spiritual strength to face their own fears, mortality, and suffering. Against all odds, they have found a heart that can love others as much, if not more, than they love themselves.

The root of this heroic quality of mind is cutting through all attachment to self and personal identity, which frees up our minds and hearts to truly care for others. Implicit in this cutting through is an acceptance of death: our own death and the death of others. If we are constantly preoccupied with maintaining what we have, we will never truly be free to care for others. The acceptance of death opens our hearts and minds.

▰▷ Today reflect on the fact that acceptance of the reality of death is essential to our spiritual growth. How might that be true for you?

DAY 20

Entering the Buddhist path is like committing to a life-long research project, in which we investigate our own thoughts, habits, and reactions and what makes us begin to shut down. After all, if we are cultivating the heroic mind of a bodhisattva, nothing is off limits. We will have to face and work through every single difficulty that comes to us in life. Although rewarding, this can be a lonely journey.

➡ Today, take some time to consider your dedication to the spiritual path. Reflect on whether you feel committed to working through the difficulties that are beginning to arise as a result of your contemplative work.

DAY 21

➡ Today, think about how our society would change if we all had more awareness of our own mortality. How would your own actions change? What might it mean to live in this way?

DAY 22

➡ If you know someone who has lost a loved one recently, ask them about their experience. As they recount the details and feelings they experience, notice if you are able to stay present. How comfortable are you as they describe their experience? Can you stay present?

DAY 23

When we consider the death of a loved one, we can imagine all of the different ways our loved one could die: from a fever, from cancer, from a heart attack, in a car accident, while taking a walk in the park, or even in their sleep.

➡ Contemplate the death of a loved one. How can contemplating in this way increase our feelings of openness and connection toward others?

DAY 24

When we see a spiritual master or a person of great, authentic presence, we often wonder where that strength comes from. What makes them so different? They seem to have something that ordinary people do not.

This vast and loving mind comes, in part, from the acceptance of death. When we accept death, both our own and that of others, we begin to open up to the pain and suffering experienced by beings around us. We begin to make a true human connection with others.

Once we feel a connection with others, there is no stopping our spiritual growth. Based on this connection, we lose our self-centered attitude. Becoming less self-involved is the first step toward cultivating bodhichitta, a mind that truly loves others without hesitation.

Where do you feel the pull to self-involvement most strongly? How might you work with that feeling?

DAY 25

Contemplate being on your own deathbed. As you look at yourself lying there, what feelings and thoughts arise? Can you make it feel real, or do you distance yourself from the scene? What are the implications of that?

DAY 26

The great Kadampa masters of old were so certain of impending death that they never took even a single day for granted. At night, they stamped out the fire instead of leaving coals for the morning and turned their rice bowls over, since they were uncertain that they would live to eat another meal.

Today, take some time to reflect on how certain you are of your own death.

DAY 27

This morning, think, "Today may be the last day of my life." Before going to bed think, "I may not awaken again tomorrow morning." Continue this style of reflection as much as possible throughout this whole year of contemplation.

DAY 28

Not realizing we will actually die, we make plans for the future and forget about today. How many times have we put off our spiritual life to some point in the future, when we believe we will have more free time? We say things like, "I'll begin spiritual practice next year when things slow down for me. Right now, I have to focus on my career/children/ spouse…" Every aspect of our lives can seem more important than our spiritual development. We put things off until a later date, even though we cannot be sure that tomorrow will even arrive.

Today, reflect on what you are putting off for the future. How do you feel knowing that the future may never come?

DAY 29

The great master Patrul Rinpoche told this story on the nature of life and death:

There once was a poor man who became lost in the fantasy of his life. He came across a pile of barley and decided to plant it in order to earn money. Once he became rich, he thought, he would marry. Once he married, he would have a son. The poor man went so far as to name his unborn son Dawa Drakpa. However, while he was lost in his fantasy, a mouse gnawed through a rope that was holding a sack tied above his head. The heavy sack fell down and struck him dead.

☞ In what ways are you similar to the old man in the story?

Day 30

☞ Consider your plans for the future. Are you striking a balance between prudent and necessary planning, recognizing that the future is uncertain? Are you leaving for tomorrow what you could do today? Or, like the poor man who wished for a son, does your planning envelop you in a fantasy that helps you forget the inevitability of death?

Day 31

Today, we can feel grateful that we have invested our energy this month in contemplating the reality of life and death. As a result of opening up to the reality of death, we have increased our feeling of connection toward others and are ready to lay the foundation for a life-long spiritual practice. It has been difficult to face this awakening to the reality of death, but we have faced it with courage and an open heart.

☞ Take a few moments to rejoice in the effort you made during the past month. Dedicate any good that came from your contemplative practice for the benefit of all sentient beings.

Contemplating Life's Insubstantial Nature

HOW DOES OUR KNOWLEDGE of impending death change us? Do we live each day as though it may be our last, keeping our connections and relationships pure, focusing on the things that are most important? Or do we act as though death isn't a reality and try to push it from our minds? If we have really internalized the fact that we are going to die, we should begin to refocus our energy, our priorities, and our goals.

Ordinary life and pursuits are insubstantial—meaning both "not real or solid" and also "lacking worth or importance." Because, as we will explore in later chapters, every part of life is impermanent and changing moment by moment, ordinary life cannot be said to have any lasting, permanent, or solid quality. And because when death comes for us, we will be unable to use or hold on to any of the achievements, loved ones, or possessions obtained during our lives, our ordinary life can also be described as insubstantial.

But even more importantly, ordinary life is insubstantial because it does not have the potential to bring us lasting happiness while we are still alive, and death is always creeping ever closer. We spend so much time chasing after things we think will make us happy, only to find that ultimately, change and loss are inevitable. In the meantime, we have grown older, our lives have gotten shorter, and we have lost valuable time to develop our hearts and minds.

On an emotional level, do we truly believe that ordinary life does not and cannot result in lasting happiness? This month, we will reflect on our own expectations, emotional investment, and attachment to worldly life, as well as the consequences of such expectations. And although many of us believe that we have our priorities straight, we may be surprised to learn that we invest most of our time and energy in beliefs and situations that will bring us unhappiness.

DAY 1

Reflecting on the reality of death and the insubstantial nature of life can feel depressing. When we think about life's end, it may seem like what we're doing now is useless, without meaning. Actually, this is a very positive and useful feeling. The Buddhist teachings call it *renunciation*. Renunciation is the knowledge that we need to move beyond mere worldly life to find something more meaningful. If we have begun to feel a sense of renunciation, we should allow the feeling to arise and not avoid it. Renunciation can help us find the energy to fuel our spiritual practice

▱⇨ What would your life look like if you used your time differently?

DAY 2

Today, contemplate the insubstantial nature of life. Although we work hard at our jobs, working doesn't bring us ultimate satisfaction. We can have difficulty relating to our bosses, our coworkers, and our clients. We struggle to balance work with family and other obligations, and with our spiritual lives. Our hard work can go unrecognized or we may not receive the pay we deserve. We may be ambitious but still not achieve everything we wish for. And although we work hard, sometimes we feel we aren't valued enough. We can end up feeling exhausted.

▨⟹ Should work be the thing you value most in life? Reflect on how much energy you invest in work and how much energy you devote to spiritual practice.

Day 3

Today, reflect on the insubstantial nature of relationships. Relationships bring us momentary joy, but they also bring us a great amount of emotional stress and suffering. We may commit to someone who does not commit to us. Our love may be unrequited. We may care so much for another person that we neglect our own needs in an unhealthy way. We may always fall for the wrong kind of person and live out self-sabotaging patterns. Or we may find a true soul mate, marry, and spend a lifetime together, only to experience the suffering of separation brought about by sickness and death.

No matter how much we love another person, the only certainty we can have for that relationship is that one day we will separate. Although we may want to believe in the ideal of everlasting love, such a thing cannot exist in the world we live in. Relationships cannot bring us any lasting happiness; what comes together will also come apart. Expecting anything different than this will only increase our suffering.

▨⟹ Consider how much energy you invest in relationships and how much energy you invest in spiritual practice.

Day 4

Each and every day, our hopes and expectations reveal to us the insubstantial nature of life. We do good things for others that go unappreciated. We may work hard to earn money in order to send our children to college, but they don't take their studies seriously, or they pursue a field where they can't make a good living. Our children may date or marry people we dislike or who abuse them. We may have ambition for ourselves, or our loved ones, that go unfulfilled. We may have strained relationships with our parents or siblings, or we may feel we never had the family we deserved. There are so many ways in which the world we live in does not measure up to what we want it to be.

▤▷ Today, meditate on how much energy you invest in fantasizing about what life should be like and how much energy you devote to spiritual practice.

Day 5

▤▷ Think of a time that you finally got something you really wanted—a new car, a vacation, a job change and a new city to live in. How long did it take before that didn't make you happy anymore? Did you notice the same old feelings of dissatisfaction coming up, even though you had been sure it was what you wanted?

Day 6

When we avoid the reality of death, we forget how to appreciate what we have. We live in a place of dissatisfaction, chasing after something we believe will make us happy, rather than feeling content with the life that we have. Although ordinary life doesn't have the ability to bring us lasting happiness, it does give us the opportunity to experience momentary joy and express kindness and compassion for others. When we can increase our acceptance of death, we will increase our contentment and appreciation of the life we have.

▰▱▻ Reflect on a situation where you might have acted differently had you realized the truth of death. What would you have changed or done differently?

DAY 7

When we realize the certainty of death and the insubstantial nature of life, certain things fall away as insignificant and other things reveal themselves as truly meaningful and worthwhile.

▰▱▻ Today, notice the types of things you tend to worry about. Will they matter a hundred years from now?

DAY 8

We don't know anyone who has achieved real happiness. We may think to ourselves, "If only I had that relationship, that job, that life… then I would be happy." But this kind of thinking is just a fantasy brought about by failing to realize that ordinary life is insubstantial. Even winning the lottery, something that many of us believe would make us very happy, does not result in increased happiness. In fact, many studies have shown that people are more unhappy after winning the lottery than they were when they were working for a living.

▰▱▻ Today reflect on your ideas about happiness. Do you believe that your ideal of happiness can be achieved? What things do you believe would make you truly happy?

DAY 9

Genuine happiness arises from a mind that is content and has cut through strong emotions such as attachment, anger, jealousy, and arrogance. While most aspects of our lives don't have the power to bring us lasting happiness, spiritual practice can give us what no other worldly pursuit can: a mind that is content and appreciates each moment, a mind that rejoices in the happiness and well-being of ourselves and others, a mind that begins to lose interest in chasing after fantasies of happiness that can never be achieved. Spiritual practice brings us toward genuine and lasting happiness.

✏️ Take time to notice if you experience moments of contentment about what you have, or of rejoicing in the success of others. Does this feel like your ideal of happiness?

DAY 10

Great spiritual masters have shown the ability to withstand hardships that seem intolerable to ordinary beings because they realized the insubstantial nature of life.

For example, in the history of Tibetan Buddhism, there are stories of many yogis and yoginis who attained realization that enabled them to transcend the necessities of ordinary life, such as clothing, food, and warmth in the wintertime. They lived in the company of wild animals and were willing to accept any hardship that came their way. The great master Milarepa was an inspiring example of such a yogi. He lived in a cave and practiced meditation day and night and only ate the nettles that grew near his cave. Many images of Milarepa depict his face with a greenish hue because of all the nettles he ate.

In truth, none of us are like Milarepa. However, although we may not be in a place where we would be willing to give up our comfortable home and delicious food, or the company of friends and family, we can still work at loosening our attachment to worldly life. Contrary to what we may have been taught, when we focus strongly on our own wishes and needs, we actually sow seeds of unhappiness and discontent. Life always defies our expectations.

▣▷ Today, reflect on the things you are most attached to and believe you need in order to survive. How many of those things are actually necessary? What expectations do you have? Are they realistic?

DAY 11

His Holiness the Dalai Lama is a portrayal of authentic happiness. When we think of the Dalai Lama, what qualities come to mind? Likely relaxation, joy, laughter, and incisive wisdom. He also works tirelessly to help disparate parties find common ground, without being discouraged or worrying too much about his own personal needs. He faces stressful and even hostile situations with a smile. Reflecting on the example of the Dalai Lama shows us that recognizing the insubstantial nature of life can bring us greater relaxation and happiness. When we lose our strong feelings of attachment to how things should be, what we deserve, and what we need, we feel freer to deal with situations as they come.

▣▷ Can you think of other examples of authentic happiness in the modern world? What unique qualities do these spiritual beings possess?

DAY 12

Anyen Rinpoche tells this story:

Once, a wealthy businessman came to see Tsara Dharmakirti Rinpoche, my root master, and offered him a box full of money to support our *shedra*, or monastic university, in Tibet. At that time, we were very poor and did not have many financial supporters. So the gift of money was much appreciated by all of us who were worrying about the day-to-day concerns of the shedra. However, just after the businessman offered the money to Tsara Dharmakirti Rinpoche, a second student entered his room and offered him a small toy car. Rinpoche was delighted by the car! He immediately began to play with the car and pretended to drive it and spin the wheels, forgetting about the money completely. This was just one of many times that our lama showed us the importance of delighting in small things, rather than being consumed by worldly concerns.

▧▷ Today, reflect on this story about Tsara Dharmakirti Rinpoche, a great modern master of the Tibetan Buddhist tradition. Pay attention to ways you too can delight in small things.

DAY 13

Spiritual practice can help us begin to cut through our dissatisfactions and change our expectations. When a situation agitates us, we can mindfully reflect on how important that situation is in the long run. If it is extremely important to our own well-being and that of others, we should attend to it with a calm and clear mind, recognizing that being upset or agitated will actually make the situation worse. However, much of the time we will probably find that the things that agitate us have to do with our own attachment to comfort and preferences. We become agitated because we don't have control over our environment, the people around us, and our loved ones. We want things to go a certain way but they don't. When we notice that we are agitated because of something that simply has to do with our own wishes, preferences, and sense of control, we should cultivate a sense of willingness to let go of that strong expression of self—what the Buddhist teachings refer to as letting go of "self-attachment."

✏️➤ Today, notice what situations cause you agitation and dissatisfaction. How important are each of those situations? Are you willing to let go of any of your wishes and preferences to preserve your own peace of mind?

DAY 14

Anyen Rinpoche tells another story:

Tsara Dharmakirti Rinpoche taught his students about contentment through his daily actions. Before we had an actual building for the study of the Buddhadharma, Tsara Dharmakirti Rinpoche and a group of thirteen monks and lamas, including myself, lived together in the wilderness with very few possessions or comforts. At first, we all lived in earthen huts that were dug in the ground, with earthen walls and leaky tarpaper roofs to keep out the snow and rain. But after a while, we monks and lamas were able to build Tsara Dharmakirti Rinpoche a small wooden hut to live in. It was much more comfortable than the dugout rooms we lived in, which were cramped, damp, and cold. However, after we offered the room to our precious lama, he often came to my earthen hut to practice, eat, and rest. He said he preferred it to the larger, more comfortable one we had built for him. We normal beings are always looking for something better, but not our lama. He was an example of perfect contentment, because he knew that true happiness comes from spiritual development.

✏️➤ Today, reflect on this story about Tsara Dharmakirti Rinpoche—and reflect on where you look for true happiness.

DAY 15

All spiritual practice starts with an excellent motivation, a positive seed in the mind. So often, when we see the dissatisfactory nature of life around us, we focus on ourselves and our own feelings. We are unwilling to move beyond ourselves and what we want, and instead we cultivate a positive feeling toward whatever we are doing at the moment. Having an excellent motivation can help us bring joy and positive energy into any situation. No matter what feelings we may have about what is happening, our positive motivation can carry us beyond those personal emotions and connect us with our greater spiritual intentions.

Today, begin to notice the motivation that comes to mind when a situation pleases you. What about a situation that makes you unhappy, sad, or angry?

DAY 16

When the motivation is excellent, the journey and result will be
     excellent.
When the motivation is negative, the journey and result will be
     negative.

Having an excellent motivation goes beyond mere optimism. When we have an excellent motivation, we are willing to put our spiritual principles into practice, even if the cost of doing so is that we will have to face something undesirable in the short-term. We make a wish of happiness for all involved, and then we do our best to engage in situations without attempting to control the outcomes. When we see the insubstantial nature of life, aware that our ideal of happiness isn't really possible, no matter how much we try to make it so, we become more willing to cultivate an excellent motivation that wishes happiness for all.

➠ Today, reflect on this aphorism from the Tibetan Buddhist tradition. In what ways can you see that results eventually ripen in accordance with your motivation?

DAY 17

The Tibetan Buddhist tradition teaches that the mind is the king of our words and actions. That is why we place the utmost importance on the quality of mind and motivation; our state of mind directly influences our body language, the energy of our presence, the way we speak, what we say, and how we engage with others. If the mind is relaxed, for instance, this quality of relaxation will be carried out into everything else we do.

The primary ways we begin to bring relaxation to the mind are by reflecting on the insubstantial nature of life and by cultivating an excellent motivation. These two forms of mind training bring positive energy and enhance our flexibility, both as we begin to lose our conviction that the happiness we wish for is actually possible and as we widen our focus to include others and not only ourselves.

➠ Today, notice how you speak and behave when your mind is relaxed. How about when your mind is tense or agitated?

DAY 18

➠ Today, challenge yourself to drop your expectations right in the moment. As soon as you notice yourself invested in the outcome of a certain situation, try to bring an excellent motivation to mind, and relax. Are you able to drop your expectations? Does the feeling of agitation linger or can you relax?

DAY 19

Our perception of every situation depends on the quality of our motivation. If we have a selfish or self-involved motivation, we are more likely to view the situation and its outcome in a narrow-minded and unhappy manner. For example, if we want to be put on a certain project at work, but instead the project is given to someone else who we feel is undeserving, we could feel extremely dissatisfied with our job and carry negative energy and feelings to the office with us. As a result, we feel miserable, and we also share that misery with others who are around us. However, if we drop our expectations for our job, realizing that job responsibilities are insignificant in the long run and don't have the power to bring us true happiness, we are free just to focus on the task at hand. We can cultivate a positive feeling in the mind, which we ourselves can enjoy and share with others.

By bringing your full attention to it, enjoy doing a task well, and share your energy of contentment with the others around you.

DAY 20

Spiritual development is always connected to motivation. In our ordinary lives, our primary motivation is usually to get what we think we want. However, after having spent some time reflecting on the insubstantial nature of life, we may have begun to realize that what we think we want usually doesn't make us happy.

So how do we help ourselves? We can achieve true happiness by benefitting ourselves and others. Here, benefitting ourselves means realizing the insubstantial nature of worldly life, shedding our hopes and expectations, and increasing our emotional stability. Benefitting others means reaching out to them and doing what we actually can to increase their well-being.

➡ Today, reflect on the connection between benefitting yourself and benefitting others. Does benefitting yourself have to get in the way of benefitting others, or vice versa?

DAY 21

Helping others is the key to happiness. This Buddhist idea is now being expressed through many scientific studies and even appears as part of popular culture. When we focus on others, we lose focus on our own expectations and dissatisfactions. We feel more connected to others and less invested in our own point of view.

➡ Today, spend some time either on the internet or at the library and read a few articles on studies that show how helping others makes us happier. Do you believe that helping others helps you?

DAY 22

Helping others is the key to happiness because by helping others, we indirectly help ourselves. If self-attachment and self-involvement are actually the cause of all suffering, then the only way to cut through suffering is by becoming less self-attached. For that reason, we say that working for the benefit of others is like a wish-fulfilling gem. Although this world is insubstantial and cannot bring us lasting happiness, still it gives us innumerable opportunities for complete spiritual transformation when we focus on the well-being and happiness of others and give up our strong focus on our own wishes and expectations.

➡ Today, reflect on the idea that all spiritual development can be accomplished by focusing on the well-being of others. Either intellectually or emotionally, is this idea difficult to accept? If so, why?

Day 23

It is difficult to focus solely on the happiness of another while completely putting aside our sense of self and expectations about the world or specific situations. However, ordinarily we find that when our own agenda is involved, it spoils what we're trying to do for the other person.

➡ Today, reflect on a time that you were able to put yourself aside and focus completely on the needs of another person. How did that feel? How about a time when you were invested in the outcome? Reflect on a time when it went your way and another when it didn't. How did those feel?

Day 24

➡ Today, challenge yourself to do something completely selfless for someone else. It can be someone you know and love, or a complete stranger. Notice how focusing on the other person feels.

Day 25

Once we have begun to become aware of our motivation, we should take our reflection on our spiritual path a step further. How do we see our own personal transformation? What kind of person do we want to be?

➡ Today, take a few minutes to reflect and journal about the kinds of qualities you would like to develop as a result of your spiritual practice. You can come back to this list at the end of this year and notice how you have changed.

Day 26

▭▷ Take a moment to acknowledge your hard work so far.

Now, having reflected on the certainty of death and the insubstantial nature of life, contemplate your view of the spiritual path. Has it changed? Also, take a moment to review your notes on your goals for this year of spiritual contemplation. After completing your first two months of contemplation, have your aspirations or priorities changed?

Day 27

▭▷ How does reflecting on the insubstantial nature of life increase your motivation to practice? Take a moment to look back on the notes you wrote at the beginning of this program about your current daily spiritual practice. Have you made any changes? How has working with the daily contemplations and tasks changed your daily practice?

Day 28

One thing that we must develop as spiritual practitioners is a Dharma Vision, a plan for our spiritual development that goes beyond what we are doing right now, or even our goals for this year. The Dharma Vision is a document that we write that explains how we see our spiritual life unfolding under ideal circumstances.

Our reflections on the Dharma Vision might go something like this: If we lived long, trained the mind, and tamed the ego, what would we be like at the moment of death? Broad-minded, content, relaxed, fearless... we probably have our own personal vision for ourselves, based on the specific emotional difficulties and habits each of us have.

Although our Dharma Vision will change over time, it acts as an inner compass, a sense of where we want to go, right from the very beginning. When we first step on the spiritual path, our vision may be something like "I want to become a deeply compassionate person." Even this general idea is extremely helpful. Without it, we wouldn't know how we should focus on a moment-by-moment basis. Over time, the general wish to become more compassionate could develop into something more specific, such as, "I would like to love others so much that I would be able to give them the things I cherish most."

✏️ Start to journal ideas for your Dharma Vision. At first, your ideas might be abstract.

If you'd like more information about formally drafting a Dharma Vision, you can find it in *Dying with Confidence*.

DAY 29

All great spiritual masters have Dharma Visions. However, their conception of it is so strong, and their commitment to spiritual practice is so intense and unwavering, that they do not need to write it down.

Tsara Dharmakirti Rinpoche constantly encouraged us to have a Dharma Vision. He often gave the following advice, "If you focus constantly on one practice in your daily life, such as evoking compassion and loving-kindness for all living beings, then eventually that state of mind will effortlessly awaken within you and express naturally from your mind."

✏️ Today, notice what kinds of thoughts are naturally expressing from your mind. How many of them are negative thoughts and emotions? How many of them are about your spiritual life and spiritual practice? How many of them are wishes for all beings to experience happiness?

DAY 30

Having a spiritual friend, a person who inspires us to develop the good qualities of our heart and mind according to our spiritual tradition, is instrumental in developing our Dharma Vision. Through our deep connection with that teacher, we can begin to learn how to develop our spiritual practice and see how the practice of contemplation and meditation can benefit us if we commit to it long-term.

➯ Have you connected with a spiritual friend? Is that connection strong enough to support your Dharma Vision? If the answer is no, how can you go about seeking a stronger connection or receiving further guidance?

DAY 31

➯ Take a few moments to rejoice in the effort you made during the past month. Dedicate any good that came from your contemplative practice for the benefit of all sentient beings.

Internalizing Impermanence

IMPERMANENCE IS AN IDEA that is so simple and self-apparent that we can overlook it entirely. Although evidence of life's impermanent nature surrounds us at every moment, we often believe, or hope, that our current situation can last. We may think that if we just plan well enough and work hard enough, we can build a life worth living, a life that is strong enough to carry us through all of the pain and suffering yet to come. But this belief only points out that we have not taken enough time to develop surety in the nature of change. Even the best-laid plans will face obstacles, and hard work may not yield wished-for results. Even if we do accomplish what we set out to do, our success, by its very nature, cannot last.

When change comes, how will we face it? With an intense emotional response, such as feelings of depression, anger, resistance, or denial? Or will we be able to fall back on our knowledge of impermanence to help us through the hard times?

Developing some acceptance of life's impermanent nature helps us to reclaim some of our misused energy; we can start to see that avoiding change is futile, a waste of time. But to be truly transformative, our understanding of impermanence cannot remain in the intellectual realm. It must become part of our emotional experience. Only then can we rely upon it as an emotional and spiritual tool to carry us through the trials of living and dying. This month we will collect evidence of impermanence in the world around us, and in our own lives. We will examine our own responses to change and try to bring our ordinary knowledge of impermanence into our emotional experiences and responses.

DAY 1

➡ Take a moment and write down four or five adjectives that describe your response to change, as honestly as you can. You can come back to this list at the end of this year's contemplations and assess if any of your fundamental attitudes have changed.

DAY 2

Is change natural? If we take time to examine our response to this question, we might notice that our thoughts and feelings are full of contradictions.

In the most general sense, most of us do feel that change is natural. We personally experience the change of growth, day by day and year by year, as we mature from childhood into adulthood. Relationships become deeper or more distant over time, and they end because of separation based on circumstance, interpersonal difficulties, or death.

However, speaking more specifically about ourselves, most of the time we do not feel that change is natural. Many times, we have a visceral response to learning that unwanted change has come to a friendship, a relationship with a loved one, or our career. We may feel depressed if illness enters our lives—because we did not expect change to affect us so personally. Even a desired change, such as a job promotion or moving to a new house, can cause anxiety and emotional agitation because we will have to face a transition in our current circumstances.

▥⟩ Reflecting on these general and personal examples of change, ask yourself again if you feel that change is natural. What can you learn from this?

DAY 3

The world around us is full of evidence that life is changing moment by moment. However, we often still ignore the changes that come. Although the seasons bring changes in temperature and precipitation, which bring changes to the sky, wind, water, trees, grasses, and flowers in the environment outside, they can happen so gradually that we do not notice the small changes from day to day. Or we have become so used to such changes that they feel normal and natural, not like change at all. When frost and snow come, we might think, "Winter has come again," or "Winter has come early this year," rather than recognizing the newness of this day and this moment.

▥⟩ Today, as you step outside, notice something that helps you recognize the newness of this day and this very moment.

DAY 4

If we watch the night sky over a period of time, we are sure to see evidence of impermanence. Each night when we go outside, we might notice that the position of the stars has adjusted slightly. Or we might notice that the size and location of the moon have changed slightly from the night before. On some nights, the moon is large and full, on other nights, it is like a sliver of light, and still on others, it doesn't appear at all.

▣▷ For the remainder of this month, go outside each evening and note the appearances of the moon and stars. If you like, draw or describe the moon as it appears in the sky each night and note the time of evening that you saw it. Or perhaps on some evenings you will notice the moon and stars are not visible because of the weather or cloud cover.

DAY 5

Amazing changes have come over our planet. Whole species have come and gone, forests have turned to stone, and ocean floors have become mountaintops. Change need not even be on such a vast scale. Even the place where you live has encountered so many changes. Entire families may have lived out the sorrows and joys of their lives in the home where you live.

▣▷ Today, reflect on the changes that have occurred in the place where you live. This could be on a large scale, such as a vast geologic change, or on a smaller scale, such as the historic roots of your city, town, or home. Reflect on how all places in the world are continually changing, just like this.

DAY 6

▣▷ Today, research extinct animal species. How many extinct species have scientists cataloged? What changes came over the world to cause their extinction? How does this add to your understanding of impermanence?

DAY 7

The first step to understanding the impermanent nature of life is an intellectual understanding. The momentum and energy of impermanence in our world is so vast and powerful, and our resistance to it is so great, that we first have to simply notice it and take note of what is happening around us. Impermanence is something we can notice at any moment if we are aware of the environment around us and the quality of our own minds and bodies.

▣▷ What helps you to recognize impermanence in the world around you?

DAY 8

Sudden and transformative changes can take place in human history as well as in the physical world. For example: the abolition of slavery in the United States or the detonation of the atomic bomb in Hiroshima had transformative impacts on the human world that people might not have been able to previously imagine.

▣▷ Think of an event in history that "changed everything." How did people's way of thinking change after that event? How did that event infiltrate our culture and politics on a national or international level?

DAY 9

Reflect on the life of an influential leader, philosopher, writer, or artist in history. Often, the words and life work of an influential person are interpreted and reinterpreted based on the changes in how people think or major events happening in a given period of time, which cause a shift in cultural consciousness. Presidents often gain popularity well after their deaths for decisions that were unpopular during their lifetimes. Writers and artists often gain prestige because the meaning of their work outlives the time in which they wrote it.

▰▷ Reflect on how the reinterpretation of history is an example of the impermanence of thoughts, ideas, and philosophies at play in our world.

DAY 10

Although we may have the idea that fame can make us immortal, it is not so. Like everything else, fame waxes and wanes.

▰▷ Today, ask an older family member or friend about famous or influential people that they remember from their childhood. This may include a movie star, a television or radio personality, or a president. How much do you know about the person they describe? How has this person's cultural influence changed? Has a contemporary member of society taken this person's place in your own mind?

DAY 11

A common example of impermanence in Buddhism is a bubble on the surface of a pond. The bubble is in a constant state of motion as it slides around on the surface of the water. Then, without a moment's notice, it pops and merges back into the water.

▰▷ In what ways is your life like such a bubble?

DAY 12

A magician is never fooled by the realistic appearance of his own illusion. Because he knows the trick inside and out, the magician may delight in the appearance he creates, but he never believes it is actually true in the way it appears to others.

▭▷ Today, reflect on how all of life is like a magician's illusion.

DAY 13

Our lives change just like the weather, based on the environment at that moment. For example, when rain clouds are present, the sun is dimmed and rain may fall. But when the same droplets of rain meet with the condition of sunlight, rainbow light displays.

▭▷ Contemplate how all of life is an impermanent expression of causes and conditions that have come together at an exact moment, in an exact way.

DAY 14

From the outside, a waterfall looks like a continuous stream of water. However, if you stand beneath the waterfall, you can feel individual drops of water hitting your face. No two drops of water are the same, although all of the water happens to flow in the same stream.

▭▷ Think of some ways your life is like the falling drops of water that comprise a waterfall.

DAY 15

Even family relationships are impermanent. When we are children, we rely on our parents completely. We can remember times when our small hands and bodies were held in their loving care, and we felt safe just being with them. As we grow older, we begin to see our parents as human beings, who are facing their own trials and difficulties, and who are growing older themselves. As we watch them age, we cannot help but notice how much we, too, have changed.

▱▷ Reflect on the impermanent nature of your relationship with your family. How has your relationship with your parents changed as you've grown older and moved from complete dependence on them to independence?

DAY 16

▱▷ Recall a close friend from childhood and the connection you had with them. Now, in adulthood, do you still have a connection with that person? How has that connection changed over the years? If you are no longer connected with them, what caused the separation?

DAY 17

▱▷ Revisit the street you grew up on, either in person, by reviewing photographs sent by a loved one, or by using the internet. What has changed in the years since you lived there? Have the new owners of your childhood house painted it a different color or planted a new tree? Does the house look smaller to you than it did when you were a child? Has the area around the neighborhood changed?

Day 18

Look at photographs of yourself over the years. Although you are the same in many ways, you have certainly been changing day by day, moment by moment, all along.

➡ As you look through the photographs, reflect on memories from that time in your life. What personal changes in you were occurring at the time of each photograph?

Day 19

➡ Now, try to envision yourself getting older and approaching death. What changes do you see in your physical appearance? Your emotional state? When you think about all the ways you have changed in the past, do you find it difficult to predict the changes to come?

Day 20

➡ Reflect on loved ones, family, and friends who have died. What caused their deaths? Recognize that just as their lives were impermanent and ended in death, so will yours.

Day 21

It's not just major life events that teach us about the impermanence of our own lives; we also know that life is impermanent because of the fleeting nature of our own thoughts, which are constantly flowing one after another, skipping from one thing to another.

▣⇒ Today, as often as possible, notice when a new train of thought begins in the mind. Recognize it as evidence of life's impermanent nature.

DAY 22

▣⇒ Write in your journal for ten minutes without stopping. Write down the first thought that comes to mind, and every thought that follows it. When you're finished, notice how many thoughts you had in just ten minutes and how quickly your thoughts changed.

DAY 23

We may feel elated in one moment and angry or sad in the next, for no apparent reason. Our emotions are similar to our fleeting trains of thought. Although we often look for reasons to explain why we feel the way we do, it's simply their impermanent nature. Because all of life is in flux, even our emotional state of mind is in a constant state of change and imbalance.

▣⇒ Today, try to notice how emotions appear one after another, sometimes with no apparent tie to the one that came before.

DAY 24

▣⇒ Today, record in a journal how many times you notice a change in your emotional state.

Note happiness, sadness, anger, impatience, indifference, frustration, rage, and any other feelings that come up. Be sure to record them in sequential order rather than generalizing them, i.e., "I felt happy about being praised by my boss and then frustrated by my workload and then happy again about having lunch out of the office," rather than just noting that you felt happy generally.

DAY 25

Impermanence does not favor one situation or another. It does not shy away from happiness and cling to suffering, though we may wish that it did. Both suffering and happiness are impermanent and will fade. No matter what situation we find ourselves in, it is bound to change sooner or later. If we realize the equal nature of impermanence, we need not be too afraid of painful situations or cling too much to happy ones.

▰▷ Today, reflect on the equal nature of impermanence.

DAY 26

Knowing the equal nature of impermanence can make emotions such as impatience and jealousy obsolete. If we truly internalize impermanence, we can bear any situation, because we're certain it will change. Also, when we see the happiness, success, or good fortune of others, we need not have feelings of envy because there is nothing worth envying. Nothing can be held on to. Everything changes and passes away. Rather than envy, we can feel connected and compassionate toward others since we all grapple with living in an impermanent world where nothing is certain.

▰▷ Today, take a moment to observe another's situation and realize that they will experience the suffering of change.

DAY 27

When thoughts and feelings arise, they're accompanied by certain sensations in the body. Your body may feel different if you're happy, sad, depressed, angry, or sick.

▥▻ Today notice the impermanence of your body. How does your body feel right now? Check in again ten minutes from now, after an hour, before bed.

DAY 28

Because all of life, including the mind, is impermanent, realization and wisdom are possible. If we human beings were not thoroughly impermanent, we could never really change. Actually, although we find impermanence difficult to deal with in our ordinary lives, it is truly a blessing in our spiritual life. Because all phenomena are impermanent, we can abandon any of our negative or harmful habits. We can go beyond what we think we are capable of. We can learn to deal with and accept painful and difficult situations. We can develop loving-kindness, compassion, and wisdom as part of our spiritual training.

▥▻ Appreciate the opportunity of change in addition to the suffering of change.

DAY 29

Ordinarily, we react to sensory data without even thinking. We believe that our senses give us real and accurate data with which to interpret the world. However, even our sensory experiences are impermanent. All sounds, smells, tastes, sights, and feelings will certainly change. For example, we may feel agitated by the sudden sound of the phone ringing when we are focused and concentrating, but the sound only lasts a few moments and then fades away. Although we should be aware of our experiences, we should not put too much emphasis on what is happening in any given moment, as it will definitely change.

▣▷ Today, reflect on how all sensory experience is impermanent.

Day 30

▣▷ Take a few moments to rejoice in the effort you made during the past month. Dedicate any good that came from your contemplative practice for the benefit of all sentient beings.

Making the Most of What We Have

IN THE TIBETAN BUDDHIST teachings, there are many stories and instructions that point out the value of the precious human life. Indeed, life—in any form—is a wonderful gift. However, according to the Dharma, what makes life as a human "precious" is the ability to dedicate our time and energy toward spiritual development.

Ordinarily, we may feel that we value the life that we have. But how much of our time and energy do we actually use for spiritual practice? Is it our priority? Or are we just fooling ourselves, calling ourselves a dedicated spiritual practitioner while not escaping the web of ordinary life?

This month, we will examine our attitude toward spiritual practice and become more realistic about how much we actually value the life that we have. Will the amount of effort and dedication we put into our spiritual practice—and the connection we have with our spiritual friend—enable us to die confidently?

DAY 1

Recall all of the different species of beings alive in the world today—all the kinds of mammals, amphibians, snakes, fish, insects, birds, and so on—and reflect on how wonderful it is that you took birth as a human being rather than any other type of living being.

Day 2

As humans, we live in a variety of different circumstances: some in wealth, others in poverty; some with great freedom and mobility, others in very set roles. The circumstances we find ourselves in are unique and can be either uniquely supportive or obstructing to spiritual practice.

▰▷ Reflect on all of the human beings alive on this planet and on how, of all those lives, you took birth into the life you have now, with all of its unique circumstances. Which of those unique circumstances most support your spiritual development?

Day 3

Many of us grew up in homes with specific religious traditions; others of us were raised in homes without spirituality. Yet, for some reason, we are thirsty to find something beyond what we know.

In Tibetan Buddhism, we call this having a "karmic connection" to spiritual practice. In other words, the result of some good action we did in the past has ripened into our present interest in spiritual practice.

▰▷ Meditate on how many people, of all the beings on the planet, aspire to a spiritual life. What are the odds that such a seed was planted in your mind and is ripening now?

Day 4

▰▷ Reflect in detail on your own karmic connection to spiritual practice. How did it begin? How has it evolved and changed?

DAY 5

Tibetan Buddhism uses the following metaphor to describe how difficult it is to obtain a precious human life, where one is inspired to practice the Dharma:

Imagine an old blind turtle living in the depths of an ocean as vast as the universe, who only surfaces once in a century. Then imagine a single collar floating on the surface of the water. It is as rare to obtain a precious human life as it would be for the turtle to put its head through that collar.

▰▷ Which of the practices from the previous days helps you relate to your own life as a rare opportunity for spiritual development? Can you think of others?

DAY 6

▰▷ Research how many people on the planet call themselves Buddhist. Among them, how many do you imagine are really inspired to practice on a daily basis? How many have accepted the truths of living and dying, and the impermanence of life?

DAY 7

The Tibetan Buddhist teachings say that a precious human life is supported by "leisure and endowments"; they're what make practice possible. Having leisure means that we have enough time to put the Dharma into practice. Having endowments means that we have all of the support we need to practice the Dharma.

▰▷ Today, reflect on whether you make enough time to practice. What takes up the majority of your time?

DAY 8

Many of us are lucky enough to have several supportive conditions present in our lives. For example, we live in a time when the Buddhist teachings are still being widely taught and practiced. But although such teachings are accessible through books and Dharma talks, we will never make a genuine connection to the Dharma without first making a connection to an authentic spiritual friend.

The spiritual friend not only teaches the Dharma in words but also transmits and exemplifies it through his or her very being. Such a person embodies the energy and essence of the Dharma, and through our commitment to him or her, we can learn to as well. If we truly value our precious human life, we should do our best to develop a personal relationship with a spiritual friend who can help us progress along the path of Dharma.

▰▷ Have you made a connection with an authentic spiritual friend? How are you developing that connection?

DAY 9

Another metaphor that is used to describe the rare fortune of obtaining a human life is that of a beggar hunting through a heap of junk and just happening to find a precious jewel buried within it. No one would expect to find a jewel buried in that trash heap even once, and certainly no one would ever expect to find one again.

▰▷ When you reflect on our own spiritual life, how often do you genuinely feel like the beggar who has just discovered unknown riches? How might you connect more to this reality?

DAY 10

Yet a third metaphor for contemplating the rarity of obtaining a precious human life is that of a single, specific grain of sand among all of the sands in the Ganges River. Among those billions of grains of sand, how rare and precious that we have found exactly this one!

▣⇨ Have you ever had the feeling that the life you have is as rare as that single, precious grain of sand? If so, when? If not, what keeps you from feeling this way?

DAY 11

Another endowment that helps us on our spiritual path is a sense of trust and faith in the Dharma. Without feeling confident that practicing the Dharma enables us to thoroughly transform our hearts and minds, we will not have the motivation and enthusiasm to practice consistently. Additionally, we need to develop confidence that practicing the Dharma during our ordinary life will ultimately benefit us at the time of death.

▣⇨ Reflect on your faith and confidence in the Dharma. Where can you see the relationship between the strength of your faith and your commitment to practice?

DAY 12

While confidence in the Dharma is important, faith must be joined with intellect. That is to say, there should be no such thing as blind faith. To use our precious human life properly, we have to think logically and carefully about what is going to happen in life.

The Tibetan Buddhist teachings describe living and dying as being carried by four great rivers: we all take birth, age, become ill, and face death. When we understand this, and live as though death is a certainty rather than something that just happens to other people, our lives become an expression of faith.

What are your feelings about faith? Is it easier for you to develop faith that is joined with intellect?

Day 13

Not only do we need trust in the teachings of the Dharma, as well as a spiritual friend to help us put them into practice, but we also need to be surrounded by a community (a *sangha*) of others who are taking up the same path.

Buddhism teaches us that we will become similar to those with whom we are close. By connecting personally with a spiritual friend, the Dharma starts to color our hearts and minds. But simply the support of a teacher is not enough. Our sangha brothers and sisters are working through many of the same difficulties we are, and we can rely on each other for support and inspiration. Especially when we are facing some of life's greatest difficulties, such as illness or death.

Have you made an effort to connect with a spiritual community? If not, what is holding you back?

Day 14

One of the greatest supports we could have during the dying process is to be with those to whom we have spiritually connected. We have no idea when or where we will die. We do not know if our spiritual friend will be present. Actually, it is much more likely that some of our Dharma brothers and sisters might be present for us, and that we could do the same for them. Connecting with a sangha helps us to make the most of the life we have now, not only as we grow together during our lifetimes, but also because we have the opportunity to support each other during the experience of dying.

▰▻ Have you considered who in your spiritual community might support you at your time of death? Are you working to deepen your connections with these individuals?

Day 15

One way to express the value of the precious human life is by making great effort to master the bodhisattva path. In the Tibetan Buddhist tradition, a story is told of the great master Patrul Rinpoche. Although Patrul Rinpoche was a completely realized being, still he received teachings on *Shantideva's Guide to the Bodhisattva's Way of Life* over and over again, all throughout his life. He never tired of receiving teachings— even the same teachings—or making great effort for the benefit of sentient beings.

▰▻ What does it look like to truly value the precious human life? To tirelessly practice the Dharma?

Day 16

The best reason to practice the Dharma today and every day is the knowledge that right now we have a precious human life—and that we may not live to awaken again tomorrow.

▭▷ Today, as many times as possible, bring to mind a feeling of uncertainty that life will continue on to the next moment.

DAY 17

If we value the supportive conditions we have in our lives right now, the best way to ensure that they will continue is to share what we have with others. When we give away what we cherish most for others' happiness, we plant seeds for good fortune to come our way in the future. That is why one of the best ways to value our human life is to practice generosity: giving of our wealth, our time, and our energy.

▭▷ Share something you cherish with others.

DAY 18

If we reflect deeply on life's impermanent nature and on the value of the human life that we have, we begin to develop ever-deepening renunciation. Renunciation is a feeling of dissatisfaction with ordinary, worldly life—but it goes beyond ordinary dissatisfaction. When we have renunciation, we realize that any attempt we make to find happiness based on worldly life will be fruitless, and that the only way to find lasting happiness is based on practicing the path of Dharma.

▭▷ Today, examine your own mind. Have you begun to develop a sense of renunciation? In what ways are you still hoping that worldly life will bring you happiness and gratification?

DAY 19

We are invested in worldly life in so many ways. Some aspects of our attachment to worldly life are obvious: food, a comfortable home, friends and loved ones, and sensory pleasures. But we are even attached to things that bring us displeasure and suffering, such as painful emotions like anger, resentment, and jealousy, and extreme behaviors such as addiction. In order to make the most of our human lives, we will have to start to gain a sense of just how overwhelming our attachment to ordinary life is.

☞ Make a list of your strongest attachments to worldly life. Be honest with yourself.

DAY 20

What distracts you from making the most of your precious human life? Do you put too much attention on work, money, family, the internet, food, alcohol, shopping, exercise...?

☞ Can you set aside a period of time for spiritual practice each day when you are willing to put aside all of these distractions? How strong is your commitment to do so?

DAY 21

Human beings have many special and unique qualities. Unlike other creatures, we can read, communicate, and use language. We are capable of being taught the Dharma and of putting the Dharma into practice exactly as we are taught. In a future life, if we do not take birth as a human being, we will not have the chance to practice the Dharma.

▆▆▷ Today, contemplate some of the unique and special qualities of human beings and how they can aid with your spiritual progress.

Day 22

All beings have natural love and compassion for their young. But human beings have the ability to train in love and compassion and to extend impartial love and compassion toward each and every sentient being.

▆▆▷ Today, reflect on your willingness to train in impartial love and compassion toward others.

Day 23

Contemplating the invaluable life that we have can be food to help us pursue our Dharma Vision: our road map for our spiritual journey. If we truly wish to die confidently, we will have to develop renunciation and put some energy into practice while we are healthy and have the chance.

▆▆▷ Today, take some time to reflect on the Dharma Vision notes that you began journaling in month 2. Make some additional notes in your journal.

Day 24

Our effort and commitment are the measure of how much we value our precious human life. It is said that if we have unwavering effort and commitment toward the Dharma, our capacity to practice and our realization will gradually increase, day by day, like the waxing moon. If we only make mediocre effort toward the Dharma, our capacity to practice and realization will gradually increase month by month or year by year. But if we make no effort at practice, we remain just as we are now. We are a self-fulfilling prophecy.

▨⇒ Try to determine, honestly but without judgment, the level of your commitment.

Day 25

What kind of practitioner do we see ourselves becoming? As we face the experience of death, what are our expectations for spiritual practice? Is it our goal to attain realization through the dying process?

▨⇒ Is the effort you are making at the Dharma right now enough to help you embody your Dharma Vision?

Day 26

▨⇒ Today, take some time to formally draft your Dharma Vision, using the notes you made in month 2. Now that you have reflected on where you see your spiritual practice taking you throughout your life, start to write down all of the support, good conditions, and personal commitment that it will take to achieve this vision. After you're done, put it aside for review at the end of the year. At that time, you may notice that some revision is in order. It's a good idea to revise your Dharma Vision each year.

DAY 27

If we use our human life wisely, we will be free of regret at the time of death. If we practice each day, do our best to embody the meaning of the Buddhist teachings, and follow what our spiritual friend teaches us, there will be no reason for regrets when the end of life comes.

Being free of the causes of regret is something we must strive for on a daily basis. Whatever harms we cause, we should apologize and make reparation the best we can. When we make a mistake, we should commit to avoid the same mistake in the future. Whenever we do good for another, we should rejoice and attempt to repeat the same behavior.

▣⇒ Reflect on what you have done today, both positive and negative. Are you free of regret about your thoughts and actions?

DAY 28

When we properly value our human life, we don't put off until tomorrow what we can do today. In spiritual life, as in all other endeavors, we will not make any progress without hard work, determination, and effort. Our positive attitude, as well as willingness to change, will help us to see our Dharma Vision through.

If we think that we will commit to practice at some future time, when we have more leisure or money or opportunity, we are just fooling ourselves. No one knows when his or her life will end, and this life that we cherish so much will burn out like the flame of a candle. Thinking this, we should make effort at the Dharma each and every day.

▣⇒ Reflect on what your Dharma effort for today will be.

DAY 29

▤▷ Today, review your Dharma Vision. Commit it to heart, either in full or in distilled form, and raise your own sense of courage and enthusiasm to see it through. Keep it in a place where you are sure to review it from time to time.

DAY 30

▤▷ Take a few moments to rejoice in the effort you made during the past month. Dedicate any good that came from your contemplative practice for the benefit of all sentient beings.

Accepting Pain and Difficult Circumstances

WITHOUT FULLY UNDERSTANDING and emotionally accepting the nature of the world we live in, we will never die confidently. We will always be too invested in ordinary life, and in our belief that ordinary life can bring lasting happiness, to be able to dedicate ourselves to spiritual practice. In Buddhism, we call the ordinary, material world *samsara*, or cyclic existence; we wander habitually through samsara from lifetime to lifetime, acting out the same old painful patterns.

m, it is taught that the very nature of samsara is suffering, e is no escape from suffering in samsara. Yet most of us re lives attempting to escape. By distracting ourselves with elf-made drama, drugs, alcohol, family, work, and all sorts lly obligations, we whittle away at the time we could be evelop our spiritual practice. This month we will examine amsara, as well as how much time we spend attempting to avoid the unavoidable experience of suffering.

DAY 1

Today, spend some time reflecting on the four great rivers, which were previously introduced—the truths of birth, aging, sickness, and death—all of which have or will certainly come to you.

Day 2

Do we believe that suffering is inevitable? When we think about our own life, do we believe that we will also experience the sufferings of aging, sickness, and death? Or do we subscribe to more ordinary views, such as the hope to "age gracefully" or "die peacefully"?

➯ Take some time to examine your thoughts about suffering.

Day 3

➯ What kinds of suffering have you experienced in your life? What is your reaction to the idea that the nature of the ordinary world is suffering? Do you believe that lasting happiness is possible if you continue to live in the same manner you always have?

Day 4

➯ When you look around you, do you feel that other beings are also suffering? Or does it seem that others have things generally easier than you do? What kind of experiences do you imagine others are having on a daily basis? Does it seem believable to you that all beings are experiencing suffering?

Day 5

This world is full of all kinds of living beings, all of whom are being carried by the four great rivers. We may idealize certain kinds of beings, thinking that they suffer less than ourselves. Poets often use birds as a metaphor for freedom, and we may have fantasies that there are other types of beings who are able to fly away from their troubles, or escape suffering by being simpler, less materialistic, and less emotional than we are. However, because we are all carried by the four great rivers, all beings are equal in the eyes of suffering.

✏️ Does it feel true to you that all beings are equal in the eyes of suffering? Why or why not?

DAY 6

Buddhist teachings say that all sentient beings are constantly being afflicted by three kinds of suffering. The first type is the *suffering of change*. We constantly suffer because life is impermanent and cannot remain the same, no matter how much we wish it to be so. We experience the suffering of change in great and small ways—the ending of a joyful moment or the passing of a loved one. We also experience the suffering of change through emotional states of mind like anxiety, fear, and hopelessness, when we anticipate change even before it happens.

✏️ Today, take some time to notice when you experience the suffering of change.

DAY 7

The second type of suffering experienced by all sentient beings is the *suffering of suffering*. This refers to the fact that sufferings are heaped one upon another. Merely because we are dealing with one difficulty does not stop another one from occurring.

Another way to understand the suffering of suffering is that physical suffering becomes mental suffering and mental suffering becomes physical suffering. For example, if the mind is filled with anxiety, we might have physical symptoms such as a stomachache or a higher respiratory rate. Or if we break our arm, we might feel emotionally vulnerable.

▣⇒ Today, take time to notice when you experience the suffering of suffering.

DAY 8

The third type of suffering experienced by all sentient beings is called the *all-pervasive suffering of conditioning.* "All-pervasive suffering" means that all sentient beings in all six of the traditional realms of Buddhism experience suffering—even those in the god realms. Birth, no matter where, entails a corporeal body, which will be the basis for the ripening of suffering due to past conditioning and will plant seeds for future suffering.

▣⇒ Contemplate the idea that even beings who take birth in the god realms will experience suffering. How do you feel about this idea? Does it deepen your conviction in the idea that all beings experience suffering?

DAY 9

▣⇒ Having taken some time to reflect on the three kinds of suffering, have your ideas about suffering changed? Has it become easier to recognize that other living beings must be suffering in a similar manner as yourself?

DAY 10

We often idealize people who are part of a certain culture, usually one that's different from ours. For example, if we grew up in an affluent society, we might believe that living in a poor country brings more happiness and less suffering, due to what we perceive to be their simpler way of life. Likewise, many people growing up in poverty believe that wealth holds the key to happiness. Such is the nature of samsara: even though we are all suffering, we honestly believe that others have escaped the sufferings of life. But because we all live in samsara, all of us are equal in our suffering.

▰▷ Do you idealize a different culture or society, believing that the people who live there suffer less?

DAY 11

Suffering arises equally from all circumstances. Many of us believe that "if only" we had something different we would suffer less. Many of our "if onlys" go all the way back to childhood. "If only she had loved me enough…" or "If only I hadn't made that choice…" In truth, suffering is inevitable.

▰▷ Today, take some time to make a list of your "if onlys" in your journal. What do you believe would alleviate your suffering?

DAY 12

Many of us are stuck in our "if onlys." They become a source of regret, a yearning for something we do not, or cannot, have. If we wish to die confidently, we cannot be emotionally stuck in regret, wishing that reality were different. When we contemplate the nature of samsara, we are better able to accept life as it is now. We become more willing to see things as they actually are rather than how we'd like them to be.

▣▷ Do you have regrets in life that you are unwilling to let go of? Take a few minutes to journal about your regrets, and why you are holding on to them. What might it mean to let them go? What would it take?

Day 13

People experience suffering according to their circumstances. For example, if we are wealthy, we experience the suffering of wealth. If we are poor, we experience the suffering of poverty. If we are famous, we experience suffering based upon that. If we are educated, suffering also arises based upon that. No matter what circumstance we can think of, it will be the cause or condition for suffering. In this way, all beings are equal in their experience of suffering.

▣▷ What kinds of suffering can you see in circumstances the same or different than yours?

Day 14

Sometimes we think that a certain change in our circumstances will solve our problems. For example, many of us believe that being independently wealthy would alleviate our suffering.

▣▷ What do you believe can cure suffering and bring happiness?

DAY 15

One of the most painful experiences we can have as human beings is to think that we are alone in our suffering. Oftentimes, we look at others around us who seem happy and satisfied with their lives, and we wonder why we are so unhappy when others seem to be doing fine. When we fall into this trap, we exacerbate our ordinary suffering with our feelings of isolation.

▰▱▷ Take a moment to contemplate the nature of samsara and to remember that all sentient beings are being carried by the four great rivers and experiencing three kinds of suffering. Use this reflection to help put aside your feelings of isolation and reconnect your heart and mind with others.

DAY 16

We may believe that we hate to suffer, but many of us are attached to feelings such as sadness, loneliness, vulnerability, anger, and resentment. Not only are these feelings deeply ingrained in our minds, but we can also rely upon them to know who we are and to feel alive. If we deeply identify with a particular experience of suffering, we may feel that we will no longer exist if we let that experience go. For example, if we felt abandoned in our childhood, we often live out that same feeling in our current relationships—not knowing what our life would be like if we felt secure. The ego invents all kinds of reasons to keep us stuck in our habitual state of mind, such as self-protection, or a need for predictability. If we are unable to see through the ego's tricks, we may waste precious time reliving the same old experiences again and again.

▰▱▷ In what ways are you attached to your emotions or experiences of suffering?

DAY 17

When we fail to realize that all sentient beings are suffering just as we are, we put distance between ourselves and others. We feel different and unique, and our suffering also feels unique. Losing our sense of connection with others is another layer of suffering that can pile up on top of the suffering we already feel buried beneath. We lose the ability to reach out to others and to realize that others can help us through difficult times.

⬛➡ Do you have the habit of withdrawing from others? How does the act of withdrawing make you feel?

DAY 18

Exaggeration is yet another trick our ego can play upon us. Although we may realize that others are also suffering, still we might feel that our pain is somehow worse than that experienced by others. For example, when experiencing the death of a loved one, we may think that we are suffering more than others do because we had a special connection with the deceased. Exaggerating our own suffering, or making it more special than the suffering others feel, is just another way that we disconnect and isolate ourselves from others.

⬛➡ Consider a time when you were certain that your suffering was unique, or uniquely intense, that no one else has suffered in that way. Reflect on whether this was truly so.

DAY 19

True dedication to spiritual practice results in the giving up of our identity. When we dedicate ourselves to the welfare of others, we lose our grip on who we think we are and what we think we need in order to survive. We constantly push ourselves past our own limits in order to serve others and the greater good. Many of the limits we set for ourselves were created based on a fear of suffering and a fear of the unknown. Authentic spiritual practitioners open their minds past these limits, attempting to live life beyond them.

✐ What might it mean to live as if you'd let your limits and boundaries go?

DAY 20

Part of our misconception about the sufferings we experience in life is the idea that they are caused by outer circumstances. Our "if only" mentality is related to this mistaken way of thinking. We often wish that things could be arranged in a way that suits us, so that we can get what we think we need to be happy. But actually, no matter how perfectly we might arrange the world and people around us, we would still find a reason to be discontent. Why is this? Because it is not possible to escape the suffering of samsara by manipulating outer circumstances. The only way to change the experience of suffering is to relax the mind and let go of negative thoughts and emotions through serious training in spiritual practice.

✐ Today, take some time to jot down a short list of things you would like to change about your life in order to be happier. For example, many of us wish to work less, have more money, have more free time, have a happier marriage, and so on. Are you willing to believe that none of these things can truly cause you to be free from suffering?

DAY 21

The great masters of Tibet are often described as being fearless and carefree—which may not be the attitudes we think we're cultivating when we pursue a contemplative practice. However, if we begin to let go of our personal identities and the attachments we have to the positive and negative circumstances and situations that have occurred in our lives, we are naturally freed from anxieties and worries. Once the mind has put aside its hopes for how things should be and its fears about how things might actually be, it relaxes, and we feel at ease in ourselves and the world we live in.

✎▷ Is your idea of happiness the same as being fearless and carefree?

DAY 22

If suffering doesn't come from outer circumstances, where does it actually come from?

The Buddha said that suffering originates in our afflictive emotions: our deeply ingrained ways of thinking and relating to the world and beings around us. For example, if we have a strong tendency toward anger, then we will experience suffering related to that emotion—heat and agitation in the abdomen, impatience, and a mental state that wishes to harm another. We will also experience the suffering that results from the expression of anger, as we must repair the damage to our connections that results from our actions, or witness ourselves causing hurt or pain to another. The expression of anger also destroys our own peace of mind and sense of equilibrium.

✎▷ What is your strongest emotional tendency? Do you like this aspect of yourself?

DAY 23

Knowing that the nature of samsara is suffering is the basis for all Dharma practice. Once we realize that all beings are suffering just as we are, we no longer need to be preoccupied by fantasies that others are happy when we are not, or that there is some way to manipulate outer circumstances so we can find happiness. We are free to pursue a discipline that can help us to tame and eradicate our afflictive emotions, the true origin of suffering. Once we do this, we are on the true path to dying with confidence.

▶ Today, contemplate your connection with specific other beings, through your mutually shared experience of suffering.

DAY 24

▶ How do you attempt to distract yourself from the sufferings of life? How much of your free time is taken up by these distractions?

DAY 25

Once we begin to awaken to the fact that the nature of samsara is suffering, we need to deepen our certainty and conviction in this truth. Otherwise, the knowledge that the nature of samsara is suffering will not be able to offer us any support when times are tough. When we are facing a difficult or painful situation, if we can bring to mind the fact that suffering is the nature of the very world we live in, we will find it easier to accept and work with the current situation.

▶ Continue to bring the nature of samsara as suffering to mind when you notice feelings of both happiness and discontent.

DAY 26

Knowing that the nature of samsara is suffering is the basis for renunciation: the wish to turn away from ordinary, worldly life and focus on spiritual practice. If we wish to die confidently, we must further develop the quality of renunciation or else we will not untangle ourselves from the distractions, fantasies, and sufferings of everyday life. We will never have enough time to develop a Dharma Vision and put it into practice.

▥▱⊳ Is your sense of renunciation increasing? Or is renunciation something you are only catching a glimpse of through intellectual understanding? How willing are you to give up your investment in ordinary life?

DAY 27

Deep certainty that the nature of samsara is suffering kindles discipline and diligence toward spiritual practice. Once we are sure that there is no way to manipulate circumstances around us to make us feel happy and content, we feel more willingness to develop a consistent spiritual practice.

▥▱⊳ How is your daily practice going? Do you put aside practice in favor of entertainment or distraction?

DAY 28

Daily practice is the first step toward dying confidently; in order to do so, we have to mingle our minds with the Dharma. That is the only way we will be sure to recall our spiritual practice at the time of death. When we work with daily practice, we bring our mind closer to the Dharma and increase our capacity to practice over time.

☞ Reflect on the ways your mind has changed over the course of these three months of reflection. How has your practice changed?

DAY 29

☞ Today, take a few moments to go back and reread some of the first entries included in this month's contemplations. Have your views about suffering changed? Do you believe that others are suffering in a similar manner as yourself? Have you loosened your hold on some of your fantasies, idealizations, and "if onlys"?

DAY 30

The Buddhist teachings say that the practitioner who has renunciation will move from "happiness to happiness." Through renunciation, we can give up our strong attachment to worldly life and focus on the Dharma, which brings us true happiness, because it enables us to eradicate our afflictive emotions and self-attachment—the true cause of suffering. Our life-long Dharma practice enables us to die confidently, which brings future happiness as we continue our work on the bodhisattva path in future lifetimes.

☞ Today, make a strong aspiration to take up the bodhisattva path not only in this lifetime but in all future lifetimes, until you reach enlightenment.

DAY 31

Take a few moments to rejoice in the effort you made during the past month. Dedicate any good that came from your contemplative practice for the benefit of all sentient beings.

Training in Virtuous Conduct of Body, Speech, and Mind

IT IS IMPOSSIBLE to die confidently without having trained diligently in virtuous conduct. Whatever habits we develop during our lifetime will be with us at the moment of death. If our hearts and minds are filled with emotional agitation and negativity during our lifetimes, then we are sure to have the same experience at the moment of death.

The Buddhist teachings describe ten types of virtuous conduct, all of which we must make effort to master in our daily lives in order to purify our negative habits and patterns. However, the key to mastering virtuous conduct, like any practice of meditation, is mindfulness. Without mindfulness, we will not notice when we have chased after and grasped on to a negative thought or emotion. Without mindfulness, we will not have the opportunity to change the course of our mental and emotional energy. And without mindfulness, we will not recognize the signs of death, nor see the stages of dissolution in ourselves, an entrusted Dharma friend, or a loved one whom we would like to support.

The next sixty days will focus on developing mindfulness, especially as it relates to virtuous conduct of body, speech, and mind. Once we start turning away from our normal patterns of thoughts and feelings, we will move closer toward our vision of dying confidently.

DAY 1

What is mindfulness? Many of us have ideas about mindfulness training and what it entails. Mindfulness has become part of our pop culture; it is in our schools, our workplaces, and in the news.

▤▷ Today, take a moment to reflect on your ideas about mindfulness practice. Do you feel you think, act, and speak mindfully?

DAY 2

In the Tibetan language, *mindfulness* is a compound word with two distinct parts. The first part, *dren*, means "to remember." The second part, *shes*, means "to know." These two words create a perfect definition of how we practice mindfulness. The knowing aspect of mind is like a gatekeeper, watching what appears in the mind moment by moment. The remembering aspect of mind recalls what we have been instructed to do when negative habits surface. For instance, we remember teachings that we have been given or the method to apply an antidote to the mind.

Both of these aspects of mindfulness must be present in order to truly practice mindfulness. Understood in this way, the actual quality of mindfulness surpasses a more general definition like "self-awareness."

▤▷ In your journal, take a few moments to write a clear definition of mindfulness in your own words. In what ways has your understanding of the term changed or evolved?

DAY 3

▤▷ Today, work with the knowing aspect of mindfulness when you notice your mental or emotional balance is off kilter. How long does it take you to notice when your mind is agitated? For example, if you see that you feel irritated or impatient, try to reflect back on when that emotion started to arise.

Does your mind catch your emotions quickly, or do they grow stronger for hours or even days before you notice them?

DAY 4

▷ Next, work with the remembering aspect. For example, if you notice that you have become impatient and upset, do you remember what you are supposed to do to work with that emotion?

Remember, though, that mindfulness does not merely require the recollection of contemplative instructions; it also requires the willingness to work with those instructions and let go of the emotion.

Do you find it difficult to remember the instructions for practice in the heat of the moment? Are you willing to actually put the instructions into action?

DAY 5

Practicing twofold mindfulness is difficult enough when we are alive and healthy. As we age and move closer to death, it will become more and more difficult to develop mindfulness as our minds begin to lose their agility. At the time of death, as the stages of dissolution begin to dawn, it becomes even more difficult to be mindful.

▷ Thinking this, motivate yourself to train extremely hard in mindfulness for the remainder of this contemplative program.

DAY 6

Mindfulness can help us notice the connection between feeling, sensation, and conceptual thoughts. With practice, we can see how sensations in the body give rise to conceptual thoughts and emotions, and also how conceptual thoughts and emotions give rise to sensations in the body.

▰▷ When your mind is agitated, how does your body feel? Where do you notice the change in sensation?

DAY 7

We can use mindfulness training to purify the expression of our body, speech, and mind. If we are mindful, we can use our gestures, demeanor, and energy to bring happiness to others, rather than upsetting them or making them uncomfortable. If we are mindful with our speech, we can use words to bring a feeling of peace and comfort to others, rather than speaking in a way that causes hurt or negative feelings. If we watch our own minds, we can start to notice our own negative thought patterns and reduce their expression.

▰▷ Today, pay particular attention to the way you speak to others, and to yourself.

DAY 8

The Tibetan Buddhist teachings say that the mind is the king of body and speech. This illustrates the power of mindfulness. If we were able to know what was happening in our own minds and remember to practice, we would be able to bring our actions and speech into harmony with our bodhisattva motivation to benefit others.

Today, notice how your words, your gestures, and even your energy are an expression of what is going on in your mind.

DAY 9

Mindfulness can be combined with correct action. In Buddhism this is described as avoiding the ten nonvirtuous actions and perfecting the ten virtues. These are linked and shouldn't be thought of as two separate lists; when we perfect the ten virtues we naturally abandon ten nonvirtues.

Today, take a moment to write down a list of what you believe should be included in a list of the ten virtues of body, speech, and mind. Then, as we go through each of these ten virtues over the next several days, notice whether your ideas were similar or different than what is presented in the teachings.

DAY 10

The first three of the ten virtues are virtues of the body. Of these three, the first is abstaining from the act of killing.

Today, take a moment to reflect on the pain you feel when another harms you, whether physically, mentally, or emotionally. Then reflect on how another person in the same situation would feel the same pain as you do.

Day 11

Often we think that only large actions harm others. However, we can harm others through the smallest expressions of our physical body, like our body language. If we harbor anger or resentment, our energy can agitate others and make them uncomfortable. Or if we are unhappy, we might drag others into our unhappiness by the way we act.

➡ Today, reflect on how even the smallest actions can cause pain, just like a thorn pricking your fingertip. See if you can notice one such action today.

Day 12

According to the law of karma, for every action, a result will ripen in a manner similar to the cause. When we harm others or take another being's life, for example, that karma will ripen so that we have a shorter life ourselves or perhaps frail health in either this or future lifetimes.

➡ Today, reflect on how any harm you inflict on others will ripen in you sooner or later.

Day 13

We should not only abstain from killing or harming others, but we should also help them whenever we can. Saving the lives of other beings is a great virtue. We may think that saving someone's life entails a grandiose action, but there are actually small things that we can do to bring other beings health and safety.

✏️▷ Today, consider adopting a pet from an animal shelter, or donating blood to help another through an accident or illness. What other things can you do to help bring another being to health or safety?

Day 14

✏️▷ Today, take a mindful walk. Notice what creatures are on the sidewalk or the ground beneath and around you. Be aware of them and tread carefully to avoid crushing or hurting them.

Day 15

Harmful actions arise from harmful thoughts. When we act in a way that hurts another, it is because we are expressing something unwholesome in our mind.

✏️▷ Today, notice when you have a harmful thought toward another. Are you able to notice it before you express the thought through negative conduct? Or if you act in a way that harms another, can you notice the sensation or thought that gave rise to the action?

Day 16

The greatest antidote to acting in a way that harms others is reflecting on how we ourselves would like to be treated. When we act, we should first think how we would feel if someone treated us the same way. We should notice what feelings are present in the mind, and then, keeping in mind the way we would like to be treated, do our best to treat others in the same way.

▱▷ Today, as you interact with others, try to stop and think before you act. Be aware of what you are doing, and if you are acting deliberately or reacting to a thought or feeling in the mind. What is the difference between acting and reacting?

DAY 17

The second of the virtues of the body is not stealing, or not taking what is not given.

▱▷ Today, reflect on how you feel when someone takes something that you have not given, and then think how others must feel when faced with the same situation.

DAY 18

When we lack awareness of our own actions, we often take from others without noticing or placing much importance on the act we have committed. For example, we might use a friend's shampoo or lotion without permission. If a cashier at the grocery store gives us too much change back, we might not return it. Someone might offer us a few minutes of their time, but we overstay our welcome without considering their feelings.

▱▷ Today, notice the small ways that you take things that aren't given. How do you feel when you do this? Do you notice any feeling of discomfort in the mind?

DAY 19

When we steal from another or take what hasn't been given, our karma will ripen so that we are in poverty or lack material sustenance in either this or future lifetimes.

▦▷ Today, reflect on how the act of stealing will ripen in you sooner or later. Reflect on how this karmic ripening might affect your ability to practice the Dharma.

DAY 20

Not only should we abstain from taking what isn't given, but we should also give others whatever we can.

▦▷ Today, challenge yourself to give when you notice yourself wanting to be the receiver. For example, if you are craving the only piece of chocolate cake on the table, deliberately offer it to someone else and dedicate the merit of your action for the benefit of all beings.

DAY 21

The act of stealing arises from feelings of mental poverty and greed. When we steal or take something that isn't ours, it's because our mind craves something so strongly that we overlook or minimize the impact of our negative action. We may think that the thing we are taking isn't wanted by anyone else, so it isn't a big deal. Or we may think that everyone else behaves the same way.

Although we may be able to cheat others, we will never be able to cheat death. Whatever dishonest thought is in our mind will be our greatest obstacle to the dying process.

▣▷ Today, notice when you have the impulse to take something that isn't yours. Are you able to notice it before you express the thought through negative conduct? Or if you do take something that isn't given, can you notice the sensation or thought that gave rise to the action?

DAY 22

Traditionally, the third of the three virtues of the body is to abstain from inappropriate sexual conduct, such as committing adultery. However, for our contemplative purposes, we can better think of this virtuous quality as honoring commitments.

▣▷ Today, reflect on how you feel when someone breaks a commitment they have made to you, and then think how others must feel when faced with the same situation.

DAY 23

The commitment of marriage or a long-term partnership can be one of the best conditions for mind training. When we participate in a committed relationship, we have the opportunity to compromise and put our spouse or partner's feelings before our own. We also have the opportunity to develop the bodhisattva quality of making and keeping a commitment.

▣▷ Today, reflect on your ability to compromise. Are you willing to give up things that you want for the good of a relationship? What is it about the relationship that lets you give up such things? How might you broaden this into other kinds of relationships?

Day 24

We may not be accustomed to thinking long and hard before we make a commitment. We may promise something as a social nicety, or because we don't take it that seriously; we feel we can back out of the commitment if need be. We may think that the promise we are making isn't that important, and it doesn't have the potential to hurt someone. However, when we think in this way, we are not thinking about the kind of karma and habitual tendency we are accruing. When we fail to keep our commitments in worldly life, we will also fail to keep them in our spiritual life. How will we gain the potential to die confidently if we are not able to keep our commitments toward daily practice, our spiritual friend, and our entrusted Dharma friends?

▣▷ Today, try to notice what is in your mind before you make a commitment. Are you sure you are going to follow through? Or did you make a promise without taking time to reflect first?

Day 25

Keeping commitments can be a skillful way to learn to put others before ourselves. If we commit to something that we later regret, we might consider following through on the commitment anyway in order to make someone else happy and reduce our own self-attachment.

A wonderful commitment to make to a friend or loved one is to become their entrusted Dharma friend. This is what we call people who have promised to spiritually support one another at the time of death. A small group of such close, committed Dharma friends is invaluable to someone who is serious about engaging in spiritual practice during the dying process; they can help that person carry out their spiritual wishes at the time of death.

If we have committed to be an entrusted Dharma friend, we should work hard to be at that person's bedside through the dying process, even though it may be inconvenient, difficult, and expensive for us to make that happen.

➥ Do you have entrusted Dharma friends? If so, reflect on how important it is to you that they keep their commitment to be with you during the dying process, and strengthen your own commitment to be there for them. If not, consider starting a list of people with whom you might make this commitment.

DAY 26

Being an authentic person is one of the goals of Dharma practice. We aim to express love and compassion in every situation, and we should make a commitment to be a genuine, loving human being who is there for others.

➥ Today, notice when you lose your positive motivation toward another. Try to rekindle love and compassion or a positive wish for the other person.

DAY 27

Of the ten virtues, four are related to speech. The first of those four is to abstain from lying.

➥ Today, reflect on how you feel when someone you trust deceives you, and then think how others must feel when faced with the same situation.

DAY 28

Can telling a small lie be as hurtful as covering up a large deception? It is possible that something that is of little importance to us is of great importance to someone else. Also, our words are verbal expressions of commitment.

We should be mindful of what we say before we say it. If we are tempted to express an untruth, we may want to think about not speaking in that moment, until we have had a chance to further reflect.

Today, notice if you are tempted to tell an untruth, or if you actually tell one. Can you see any positive or negative consequences for doing so?

DAY 29

What is the true motivation behind dishonesty? Often, we are unaware of why we deceive others. And often we come up with positive reasons to justify why we act the way we do. For example, we may think that we are lying to protect someone from feeling hurt. This may be true, and may be an example of a positive motivation behind dishonesty. But it is equally possible that we are trying to protect ourselves by lying. We lie in order to make ourselves look better than we are. Or we lie in order to avoid having to deal skillfully with a situation that has arisen between ourselves and another person.

Today, think of a time you have deceived another about something important. What was the result of that deception? Do you see honest ways you could have handled it better?

DAY 30

An important aspect of becoming a Dharma practitioner is being a genuine human being. Part of being genuine is having awareness of our own minds, our own habits and tendencies, and our own motivation. We may pride ourselves in being a good, honest person toward others, but the person we most often deceive is ourselves. If we deceive ourselves, how can we be honest and loving toward others? How can we make commitments without regret, and carry them through with a loving mind?

Dying confidently requires paramount honesty. At the moment of death, we will have nothing and no one to rely upon except the qualities that we have brought to fruition in our own minds. We had better know what those qualities are, and be aware of our own shortcomings, if we are to make progress at spiritual development.

▱▷ Do you feel you are honest with yourself about your positive and negative qualities? Today, notice the deceptive aspect of your self-attachment.

DAY 31

The Tibetan Buddhist teachings tell us to carry a mirror and look at our own face. This saying points out our tendency to notice the faults of others while avoiding looking inward.

Mindfulness is the best tool for noticing the fault of dishonesty. By vigilantly watching over the mind, we slowly begin to see our tendency to self-protect, one of the biggest obstacles to spiritual practice. When we self-protect, we attempt to maintain our ego, our self-attachment, rather than breaking it down. If our self-attachment remains intact, we are sure to feel fearful at the moment of death.

▱▷ Today, work with the metaphor of holding a mirror pointed toward yourself. Try to notice any impulse to deceive and self-protect. If you notice that kind of thought in the mind, attempt to relax the thought by taking several deep breaths.

Day 32

The second of the four virtues of speech is to avoid divisiveness. When we speak divisively, we attempt to put ourselves between two or more people; we attempt to separate others and destroy their intimacy or community.

➥ Reflect on how you feel when someone interferes in your connection with another, and then think how others must feel when faced with the same situation.

Day 33

In what ways do we act divisively? Do we attempt to make ourselves the center of attention? Do we use speech as a way to pull others to our own side? Do we use speech as a way to push others apart so that we have the opportunity to be the most important member of the group? Do we speak in a way that sounds kind but is intended to poison another's connection?

➥ Today, reflect on your own tendency to be divisive. In what situations have you spoken or acted divisively? How might you meet those situations less divisively?

DAY 34

When we speak divisively, the result of that karmic tendency will ripen in a similar manner. For example, in this or future lifetimes, we may become separated from our loved ones, unable to reconnect with them, for any of a host of reasons. Indeed, we may find ourselves alone and isolated even though we are surrounded by a community of people.

▰▷ Think of a time when acting divisively caused you to feel isolated. What happened?

DAY 35

Speaking divisively within our spiritual community, or in relation to our spiritual friend, is extremely grave. All members of a sangha are like fledgling bodhisattvas, and the sangha's spiritual friend is the crown jewel of them all. And when we slander a buddha or bodhisattva, the karmic ripening is very dark and heavy. By disrespecting the harmony of our spiritual community, we accrue terrible karma that obstructs our spiritual development. At the time of death, that karma may ripen as the inability to practice or as an agitated state of mind that obstructs any possibility of realization.

▰▷ Today, reflect on whether you have spoken divisively among your sangha or negatively about your spiritual friend. If you have, cultivate a feeling of regret and commit to watching this tendency of the mind.

DAY 36

The third of the four virtuous kinds of speech is avoiding harsh speech. When we speak harshly, we express anger, resentment, jealousy, pride, or any other afflictive emotions. We destroy the peace of mind of others. Quite literally, in such circumstances, our speech is a weapon.

▨▷ Today, reflect on how you feel when someone speaks harshly toward you, and then think how others must feel when faced with the same situation. How often does your harsh speech lead to a feeling of regret?

DAY 37

We may think of harsh speech only as something that is expressed when we have an extreme state of mind. For example, if we are in a heated argument, we might speak with the goal of silencing the other person or hurting them with our words. But if we are mindful and aware of how we speak, we will probably notice that we speak harshly even during our small interactions, such as to the teller at the bank when we are in a hurry or to a telemarketer who bothers us with their phone call.

▨▷ Today, start to notice the way you speak to people. Do you often speak in a way that expresses strong emotions and might hurt others? Do you feel justified when you do this?

DAY 38

▨▷ Reflect on a time when you spoke harshly or thoughtlessly. How could you have changed how you spoke? Can you think of a way to more skillfully get your point across? Or was it a case where you shouldn't have said anything at all?

Day 39

▰▱▱▻ Today, try to notice the impulse to speak harshly. When you notice it is present, look at your emotional state. What emotions are driving your speech? Are you able to stop and rethink what you were about to say? Or do you only notice that you have spoken harshly after it has already happened?

Day 40

The result of karmic tendencies ripen in a manner similar to the cause. So when we speak harshly, in this or future lifetimes we may become the object of others' ridicule or abuse. We may find ourselves incapable of communicating meaningfully with others.

▰▱▱▻ Is there a time, after you have spoken harshly in anger, where you have noticed a lasting impact on a relationship, or on yourself?

Day 41

The last of the four virtues of speech is avoiding idle speech. When we express ourselves carelessly, we may engage in conversations that create needless disagreements or heated, emotional exchanges. We may speak untruthfully or embellish a tale in order to be the center of attention. We may gossip about others in a way that sows resentment among others and reinforces negative views in our minds.

▰▱▱▻ Today, reflect on how you felt when you were the subject of idle speech, and then think how others must feel when faced with the same situation.

DAY 42

Ordinary conversation can be one of our main distractions from spiritual life. For example, even when you are with your spiritual community, how often do you debate about politics rather than focusing on practice? How often do you talk about the state of your government or your society? How often does this encourage yourself and others to express strong emotions when you should be working at training your minds?

☞ How much time do you spend talking about the insubstantial world around you each day rather than focusing on Dharma?

DAY 43

☞ Today, focus on positive speech. If someone around you is speaking negatively, try to change it into something positive with your energy and your words.

DAY 44

Many great, realized masters in the Tibetan Buddhist tradition stopped engaging in ordinary speech. Some of them never spoke at all, except to recite mantras, prayers, or blessings. Gyalgo Lama Sosang is a modern example of such a master; he stayed in retreat in a cave for more than forty years and stopped speaking entirely except to recite Avalokitesvara's mantra.

☞ Why do you think Gyalgo Lama Sosang set this example? In what small ways might this example inform your own practice?

DAY 45

▭▷ Today reflect on your conversations with others. How many of them were about something meaningful? What is meaningful speech? Do you notice that there were times you should have not entered a conversation? Today, pay close to attention to how you speak, and about what.

DAY 46

The last three virtues are related to the mind. The first of those three is avoiding greedy thoughts and coveting what another has. When we are greedy for what is possessed by others, it influences our actions, our speech, and our motivation toward that person. Our state of mind pours out of our skin, and others can feel our greedy, covetous energy.

▭▷ How do you feel when someone else expresses greedy energy toward what you have? Think how others must feel when faced with the same situation.

DAY 47

We often wish for what others have, sometimes even wishing that we had it instead of them.

▭▷ Do you believe that having what someone else has would make you happy? Having reflected at length on the nature of happiness, is there any logical reason to wish for good things for yourself, while indirectly wishing loss or suffering on another?

DAY 48

Today, reflect on the karmic ripening of a greedy state of mind. When we feel greedy for what others have, in this or future lifetimes we may become a person who possesses things but cannot enjoy them.

Reflect on a time when you were unable to derive happiness from something that you previously wanted immensely.

DAY 49

Today, notice when you feel greedy for what another possesses. What does it feel like? Is it an agitated state of mind? A heavy one? What kinds of situations cause that reaction in you?

DAY 50

Recall the Buddha's First Noble Truth: ordinary life cannot bring us happiness because the nature of this world is suffering.

Reflect on this the next time you feel greedy. Does your contemplation help you to release the feeling?

DAY 51

Today, try to notice positive things about your life. What good and supportive conditions do you have for Dharma practice? What are the good qualities of your loved ones? What makes you feel happy? When you feel content, does your mind feel less greedy? Do you find it difficult to find satisfaction with your life?

DAY 52

The second virtue of the mind is abstaining from harmful thoughts toward another. The negativity of this needs little elaboration; it causes pain for both ourselves and the target of our negative motivation.

▱▷ Reflect on how you feel when someone else has harmful thoughts toward you, and then think how others must feel when faced with the same situation.

DAY 53

When we have harmful thoughts toward another, we are in danger of being overwhelmed by our afflictive emotions and carrying out a harmful action. Even very subtle thoughts, if not caught by our mindfulness and introspection, could grow such that we are unable to control ourselves, and act them out.

▱▷ Today, reflect honestly about the harmful thoughts you have toward others. What seems to trigger such thoughts?

DAY 54

▱▷ Can you think of a time that you wished harm on another, large or small? Did you carry it out? How did it feel while you did it? How did you feel afterward?

DAY 55

At the moment of death, we will regret having had harmful thoughts. Our minds will be colored by the collective karma and energy that we cultivated during our lifetime. If we wish for a positive and open state of mind at that time, it is imperative that we abandon any harmful thoughts that come in the mind.

➡ Today, commit to abandoning any harmful thoughts that arise in the mind.

DAY 56

The last of the four virtues of the mind is avoiding wrong view. When we have wrong view, we see the outer world impurely. We are skeptical, critical, judgmental, and self-righteous. Our minds become filled with negativity.

➡ Today, examine your critical mind especially as it relates to your spiritual practice, your spiritual friend, and your spiritual community. Are you distrusting or skeptical?

DAY 57

Self-protectiveness is one of the worst kinds of wrong view. In the Tibetan Buddhist teachings, it is said that the best kind of lama is the white-hearted lama. This kind of lama loves us fiercely and is willing to point out our faults even though we often do not appreciate his or her effort and attention.

▣▷ Today, reflect on the tendency that we have to see the person who tries to help us most, the spiritual friend, as hurting us rather than offering us spiritual support.

DAY 58

▣▷ Where is wrong view obstructing your Dharma Vision? How does it impact your daily practice and ability to truly commit to your spiritual friend and spiritual path? How will this negatively impact your ability to practice at the moment of death?

DAY 59

During the dying process, any wrong view that you are holding on to will obstruct your practice. Even if a lama is beside us, attempting to guide us through the stages after death, his or her effort will bear no fruit because we are incapable of connecting with the lama through genuine faith and devotion.

▣▷ Today, make a strong aspiration to give up any wrong view you have toward the Dharma, your spiritual path, and your spiritual friend.

DAY 60

▣▷ Of all of the virtues of the body, speech, and mind, which did you find you need to work on the most? Keep it in mind during the remainder of this year and apply mindfulness and introspection to your practice of the virtues. Remember that the stronger the negative habit is, the more destructive it will be to our peace of mind at the time of death; mindfulness must be our constant companion on the spiritual path.

Day 61

▬▷ Take a few moments to rejoice in the effort you made during the past two months. Dedicate any good that came from your contemplative practice for the benefit of all sentient beings.

Going Beyond Our Limits

IN ORDER TO DIE confidently, we have to transcend our ordinary impulse to protect ourselves—to maintain the life that we have and who we think we are. At the moment of death, if there is any grasping or attachment present within our mind, we will not be able to practice; we'll experience fear when we realize all that must be let go of in that very moment. We may feel that we're most attached to individuals and phenomena other than ourselves—our loved ones, friends, homes, and belongings. However, at the very root of our ordinary existence is a deeply ingrained tendency to grasp at the self. We are obsessed with ourselves and our own experience. We are profoundly self-involved, so that it's very difficult for us to take the focus off of ourselves for substantial periods of time. When we suffer, we suffer all the more because of the amount of energy we invest in that suffering.

Developing bodhichitta, the mind of enlightenment, enables us to cut through this deep habit of making ourselves important, of always worrying about ourselves, and of feeling that our suffering is unique simply because it's *ours*. This month we will contemplate the mind of enlightenment, as well as work with techniques to help us begin to reverse our strong habits of self-grasping. By doing so, we will begin to lose our anxiety, fear, and hard outer protective shell so that we can be present, fearless, and confident at the moment of death.

DAY 1

Our contemplation of bodhichitta begins in training in what are known as the four immeasurable qualities: joy (or rejoicing), loving-kindness, compassion, and equanimity. These qualities are the basis for beginning to go beyond our self-imposed limits. Our ordinary minds are self-centered, concerned only with those that we feel close to and see as an extension of ourselves. But when we cultivate these four qualities, we are attempting to stretch our minds so as to make room for others that we normally wouldn't take the time or energy to care for—or whom we don't like and are unwilling to love or care for. When our minds are not limited by preferences and prejudices, we will let go of the fear that binds us to ordinary life and inhibits our practice at the moment of death.

▰▷ Today, take a few moments to make a list in your journal about different groups of people: those to whom you feel capable of giving your energy, those to whom you feel unwilling to give your energy, those you feel no connection toward, those you feel ambivalent toward, and so on. Try to be specific in your connections with others, and notice how the nature of your feelings affects your willingness to give of yourself.

DAY 2

When we develop the four immeasurable qualities, we begin by working with the quality of equanimity. Equanimity is the quality of seeing others as being in the same situation as ourselves and equal to ourselves in the wish to be happy and avoid suffering. It is also the quality of our own mind being free of desire and anger.

If we are unable or unwilling to see others as being equal to ourselves, we will have difficulty developing loving-kindness, compassion, and rejoicing in their happiness and good fortune.

▦➤ Today, reflect on whether you actually do see others as equal to yourself. Are there persons you love enough to treat as yourself? If so, who?

DAY 3

▦➤ Today, contemplate and train in equanimity toward a loved one. Choose the person toward whom you feel the most loving and generous. Think to yourself that your loved one wishes for the same kind of happiness you do and suffers from the same painful emotions as yourself. Try to imagine giving to your loved one the things that you love and enjoy most. What things can you mentally give your loved one? Are there things you feel you only want to keep for yourself and not share?

DAY 4

▦➤ After you contemplate equanimity toward a loved one, change the subject of your meditation to a person toward whom you feel neutral. This should not be someone you are ambivalent toward, but rather a person for whom you have neither a strong feeling of like nor dislike.

Can you share the same things with this neutral person as you can with your loved one? Can you open yourself toward the person with whom you are less intimate?

DAY 5

▦➤ After you contemplate equanimity toward a loved one and then someone you feel neutral toward, move to someone you mildly dislike or resent.

Are you able to share the same things with this person as you are with your loved one? How about the person you feel neutral toward? Are you willing to drop some of the discomfort that can come with focusing on their happiness?

DAY 6

✏️ After you contemplate equanimity toward a loved one, one you feel neutral toward, and one you mildly dislike, move to a person you have a strong feeling of resentment or dislike toward. You may feel that this person has harmed you in one way or another.

Are you able to let go of that feeling of injury and self-protection and truly feel that person is equal to yourself? Is your mind overcome with feelings that don't allow this? What kind of thoughts come to mind?

DAY 7

✏️ After you contemplate equanimity toward a loved one, a person you feel neutral toward, a person you mildly dislike, and a person you resent or dislike, try to extend the mind of equanimity to people in the city you live in, many of whom you have no connection with or have never met. Then try to extend that state of mind to encompass your whole region or country.

What is your emotional reaction? What thoughts come to mind?

DAY 8

✏️ After you contemplate equanimity toward a loved one, a person you feel neutral toward, a person you mildly dislike, a person you feel has harmed you, and those living in the same city, state, and country as yourself, try to extend that feeling toward those living in other parts of the globe, whom you have never met and may have no connection toward.

What is your emotional reaction? What thoughts come to mind?

DAY 9

✏️ After you contemplate equanimity toward a loved one, a person you feel neutral toward, a person you mildly dislike, a person you feel has harmed you, and those living in the same city, state, and country as yourself, and those living in other parts of the globe, try to extend that state of mind toward those leaders, groups of people, or cultures that you view as aggressive, oppressive, or disruptive of peace on a local or global level.

What is your emotional reaction? What thoughts come to mind?

DAY 10

Equanimity is the basis for the other three immeasurable qualities. If we don't feel that others are equal to ourselves, how can we really wish them happiness and freedom from suffering? In the traditional presentation of the Tibetan Buddhist teachings, students are taught to contemplate equanimity for a long period of time before moving on to any of the other qualities. However, in order to benefit readers with varying levels of experience, this month we will continue on to the methods for contemplating the rest of the four immeasurables.

✏️ Today, continue working with the contemplations on equanimity just described. If you're able, try to continually work with this series of contemplations in addition to the other exercises described daily.

DAY 11

▶ In what ways do you notice your contemplations on equanimity affecting your thought patterns and interactions with others? Do you notice a reduction in fear or other self-centered emotions?

How will this affect your state of mind at the moment of death?

DAY 12

The second immeasurable quality is that of loving-kindness. Loving-kindness is defined as the wish for all sentient beings to have happiness and the cause of happiness.

▶ If or when you feel you're ready to complete the cultivation of immeasurable equanimity, use the same series of contemplations that you used in days 1–9 of this chapter to cultivate immeasurable loving-kindness. For example, begin by wishing that a person to whom you feel extremely close has happiness and the cause of happiness, and so on.

DAY 13

▶ In what ways do you notice your contemplations on loving-kindness affecting your thought patterns and interactions with others?

Today, when you feel angry or resentful toward another, can you bring your contemplation of loving-kindness into the interaction and wish that person have happiness and the cause of happiness? If not, what stopped you?

Day 14

The third immeasurable quality is that of compassion. Compassion is defined as the wish for all sentient beings to be free of suffering and the cause of suffering.

▰▷ If or when you feel you're ready to complete the cultivation of immeasurable loving-kindness, use the same series of contemplations that you used in days 1–9 of this chapter to cultivate immeasurable compassion. For example, begin by wishing that a person to whom you feel extremely close is free from suffering and the cause of suffering, and so on.

Day 15

▰▷ Do you notice a difference in the level of challenge or difficulty in seeing others as equal to yourself versus wishing for their happiness and wishing for them to be free from suffering?

Why is it more difficult to wish for others to be free from suffering than it is to wish for them to simply be happy? What sorts of emotions have to be overcome in each case?

Day 16

The fourth immeasurable quality is that of joy. Joy is defined as the wish for all sentient beings to have immeasurable joy free from partiality and prejudice. It is also the quality of rejoicing in others' happiness and good fortune.

▰▷ If or when you feel you're ready to complete the cultivation of immeasurable compassion, use the same series of contemplations that you used in days 1–9 of this chapter to cultivate immeasurable joy. For example, begin by wishing that a person to whom you feel extremely close has supreme joy free from partiality and prejudice, and so on.

DAY 17

One of the best ways to practice immeasurable joy, as well as the other immeasurable qualities, is to rejoice in the happiness and success of others. When we rejoice in the good things that others possess and experience, we ensure that we're not falling into a selfish state of mind, one that wishes for us to be happier than others, have more than others, suffer less than others—a state that can only delight in the joy of those whom we love and care about. If we truly are training in rejoicing as an engaged practice, we will carry that state of mind with us all the way to the moment of death.

➥ Today, take notice of the success or comfort of another, even something as simple as a beautiful house, and rejoice that another can enjoy such a thing. Add to that the wish that everyone could enjoy that condition.

DAY 18

Bodhichitta is defined as dedicating our own root of virtue, anything positive we have, for all sentient beings to attain enlightenment. In making this wish, we also are freed from the bonds of self-attachment, since our entire focus has been placed on the happiness and welfare of others, and giving up every single aspect of ourselves in the process. Bodhichitta incorporates all of the immeasurable qualities; it's a vast, immeasurable state of mind that wishes for each and every being to attain temporary happiness, as well as freedom from suffering and the impartial joy that comes from complete realization.

Once we have realized bodhichitta, we no longer need to worry about ourselves at the moment of death; our confidence will be unshakable. As we lose the focus on ourselves and our own happiness, we also lose the cause of worry and fear. We become like the fearless, carefree yogis of Tibet.

➤ Today, evaluate how your practice of bodhichitta is going. Do you notice yourself taking more interest in others? How does this make you feel?

DAY 19

Training in the four immeasurable qualities is the method for training in *aspirational bodhichitta*. Aspirational, or wishing, bodhichitta is a contemplative point of reference that we can use constantly in conjunction with any thought or action, no matter how mundane. We can use one of the techniques associated with the four immeasurables or just make the wish that any good that comes from our thoughts and actions might benefit all sentient beings. Aspirational bodhichitta is so-called because it is a contemplative practice that can be done without any engaged action; it is a type of mind training.

➤ Today, try to recall aspirational bodhichitta as many times as possible. In the evening before bed, note how many times you were able to train in aspirational bodhichitta. Is it more or less than you were expecting?

DAY 20

➤ Today, notice how many times you express one of the ten virtues of body (not killing, not stealing, keeping commitments), speech (not lying, not speaking divisively, not speaking harshly, not speaking idly), and mind (not coveting, not having harmful thoughts toward others, not having wrong view). Each time you do, can you recall the mind of aspirational bodhichitta and wish that your virtuous activity be for the benefit of others?

Day 21

■⇒ What can you do today to inspire happiness in others? Can you use your voice, your demeanor, even your way of dress to express aspirational bodhichitta?

Day 22

Tonglen, literally "sending and taking," is a practice we can use to train in viewing others as equal to ourselves based on the four immeasurable qualities. Similar to training in immeasurable equanimity, we can begin this practice by working with a person we feel connected to, and then move to a person we feel neutral toward, one we feel mild dislike toward, and so on. With tonglen, we can rely on our training in the immeasurable qualities to be willing to take in, literally on our inhalation, the suffering of others. Then we can send out to them our root of virtue and anything positive we have, with our exhalation. Focusing on the breath this way makes the mind concentrated and calm as we also add the complementary practice of aspirational bodhichitta.

■⇒ Today, add the practice of tonglen to your training in the four immeasurables. For example, if you are training in immeasurable loving-kindness, reflect on a being experiencing a specific type of suffering. As you recall to mind the wish for them to experience happiness and the cause of happiness, breathe in and imagine that you have taken their suffering upon yourself, and then exhale your wish for their happiness. Work with the breath in this way for ten minutes.

DAY 23

We can use the practice of tonglen in our reflections on the dying process. When we encounter someone who is ill or is facing tremendous physical suffering, we can use our inhalation to take their suffering upon ourselves. In that moment, we can be willing to face the fear and suffering of death for them. Then, we can breathe out a sense of health and well-being to them.

If we find it difficult to practice tonglen, we can move back to practicing equanimity, thinking that all beings have the same wish we do to be liberated from the fear of death.

Today, practice tonglen for someone who is ill, dying, or suffering in some way, such as having lost a child or going through a divorce.

DAY 24

Today, sit down and watch the news, or buy a newspaper and reflect on some of the stories of human suffering that you see or read. Practice tonglen based on something that you connect with emotionally. Notice what is difficult about this practice. What thoughts or feelings does it bring up?

DAY 25

When we take on another's suffering, even just in aspiration, we may feel threatened or even scared. Sometimes we misunderstand the practice and believe that it makes us sick or fills us with negative energy. We should understand that all of these kinds of thoughts are simply the ego attempting to protect itself. At this stage in Buddhist practice, none of us has the actual ability to truly take on another's suffering or painful energy. Any belief that we have done so is just a trick of the ego.

Tonglen is a practice designed to destroy the ego. Remember that the ego will steal our opportunity to practice at the moment of death if we don't take the chance to break it down now.

✏ Examine your feelings as you practice tonglen. Do you feel worried or anxious? If so, recognize that those feelings are just your ego, and release them.

DAY 26

Even suffering as simple as a headache can be used in a practice like tonglen. For example, if we have a headache, a blister, or another simple kind of physical suffering, we can think to ourselves, "May I take on this suffering from everyone who is suffering in the same way as I am, since I am already experiencing it. May they enjoy peace, health, and happiness."

✏ Today, what simple form of suffering can you use to train in tonglen?

DAY 27

We often think that tonglen is a practice that helps us to benefit others. Actually, it truly benefits us. Tonglen is a practice that helps us achieve our Dharma Vision. It increases what we believe we are capable of, and increases our capacity and willingness to let go of our selfish desires. The less focused we are on getting what we think we want, the more energy we have to open up and practice the path of Dharma.

✏ Today, notice how you feel when you focus on another's suffering. When you take the focus off of yourself, what happens to the quality of your mind?

DAY 28

The practice of tonglen has two more advanced stages. The first is to exchange oneself for others. We actually train in the motivation to give up what we want and offer it to another instead. This can be very difficult to do, even with something as simple as a meal that we wish to eat or a comfortable chair to sit in. However, bodhisattvas exchange themselves for others constantly, always keeping in mind the thought that all sentient beings have the same wish for happiness and to avoid suffering.

✏️ Can you think of anyone you are capable of exchanging yourself with, offering them what you want instead of enjoying it yourself? If so, who? If not, why do you think this is the case?

DAY 29

The final stage of tonglen is to make others more important than ourselves. This type of practice is illustrated by bodhisattvas who gave up their spouses, children, or even their own limbs, for the benefit of another. The motivation behind this practice is illustrated by the prayer "all benefit to others, all loss to myself."

✏️ Make aspiration prayers to become the kind of fearless practitioner who can give all benefit to others and take all loss upon themselves.

DAY 30

✏️ Take a few moments to rejoice in the effort you made during the past month. Dedicate any good that came from your contemplative practice for the benefit of all sentient beings.

Giving of Ourselves

IN ORDER TO DIE confidently, we have to get comfortable not only with giving of ourselves but with actually letting go of ourselves—body and mind. We will have to give up everything, including the identity we cherish and all of our ideas about who and what we are. When death is just a distant thought, we may not struggle with this complete and full dissolution. But when death comes for us, intellectual understanding will not help us; it's far beyond anything we can comprehend intellectually. At that moment, we will be alone with our mind and emotions, with nothing to obscure or distract us from the experience at hand.

We should remember that, at the moment of death, we will not be able to take anything with us. No matter how precious our loved ones, our home, or our possessions are, we will have to leave them behind. And most difficult of all, we will have to witness the decline of our health and our physical selves as we age or sicken, until finally we have to leave even this body behind.

In our ordinary lives, we often cling to our wealth and possessions, thinking that by doing so, we're protecting ourselves from fearful, painful, or difficult situations. We also might have the idea that by holding on to what we have, we're creating abundance and wealth. However, we should recognize this attitude as mere mental poverty—clinging that will only bring us greater suffering in the future.

Because we believe we do not have "enough," we feel we have to tightly cling to what we do have. We hoard our love, our energy, our relationships, our possessions, and our wealth. But an attitude of mental poverty will not serve us in our lives, nor will it serve us at the time of death. We will always feel distracted and unhappy about what we lack, rather than enjoying and using what we actually have for the greater good.

Confidence in the moment of death arises from the willingness to give everything up and to face that moment with nothing.

DAY 1

We live in an individualistic society that looks down on people who put others first. We may feel that we have to put ourselves first, or no one will. Society may teach us that this is a healthy attitude, but we should recognize that we are only nurturing our ego.

Some kinds of giving probably come naturally, such as being willing to give our time and energy to others who are in pain. Can we stretch that tendency to include someone outside of our normal circle of friends and family?

What are we terrified to give? Many of us have trouble parting with money or material possessions. Could we give all of the money in our wallet to a person in need? How much of what we have are we willing to share? With whom?

➥ Today, reflect on your attitudes about giving. Think both of your natural tendencies for giving and of your fears and barriers.

DAY 2

In the Tibetan Buddhist tradition, we start the day by making an offering of water on our shrine in seven small bowls. We do this because the masters of our tradition have recognized how difficult it is to give without any attachment. In Tibet, water is free, cold, clear, pure, and abundant. It's the perfect thing to offer because it is something to which we feel no attachment. It costs very little and we can easily get more.

Often in our lives, we find it difficult to give in this unselfish way. Even when we give something small, we tend to second-guess ourselves and wonder if we should not have kept the thing we gave. Making a water offering on a small sacred table is a wonderful way to start a new habit: reflecting on abundance.

✎ Experiment with making an offering of water on an altar or sacred table each morning.

DAY 3

We come up with all kinds of excuses not to give. One of the most powerful is judgment. When we see someone who is in need of help, such as a homeless person asking for food, money, or work on a street corner, we often judge them to avoid giving. We wonder what they'll do with the money we give them. Will they use it to buy drugs or alcohol? Why don't they have a job and work like the rest of us? What have they done to get themselves into this situation in the first place? Or maybe we think they're out to take advantage of us, that they aren't really in need at all.

No matter what the particulars of the situation are, we should know that giving always benefits us. When we choose not to give, we lose the precious opportunity to chip away at our self-attachment and ego. And we lose the chance to diminish our feelings of mental poverty.

✎ Today, be willing to let go of judgment, seeing it as another expression of ordinary self-attachment.

DAY 4

The Buddhist teachings describe three levels of giving, from the most simple to the most profound. We may be surprised to learn that the easiest type of giving is that of material possessions and wealth. It's the simplest way to train in the practice of generosity and giving.

No matter what we give, we should give it without hesitation. If we're only capable of giving a penny right now with no feelings of greed or attachment, we should start by giving a penny. From there, we can work up to ten cents, a quarter, a dollar, five dollars, and so on. By starting out with something small and seemingly insignificant, we can begin to prepare for the moment of death, when we will have to leave all of our wealth and possessions behind.

▰▷ What amount can you give without hesitation? Give whatever it is to a person in need, a waiter/waitress, a jar collecting for medical research or another charitable cause, or any other opportunity you find.

DAY 5

Even more important than the act of giving is the motivation behind the act. Do you give reluctantly, impulsively, or with an expectation to receive something in return? Is your giving out of a feeling of obligation or to demonstrate, even just to yourself, how generous you are? Do you give resentfully or regret your positive act? To be truly free of self-attachment, we must get beyond all of our hidden motives and give only for another's benefit. It is important that we explore all of the mind's corners and crevices and dust off the cobwebs of self-grasping hanging there.

▰▷ Reflect on a time you gave something wholeheartedly. Remember the experience and how it felt. In what ways do you struggle to give wholeheartedly?

DAY 6

The great masters of Tibet had a tradition of offering all of their wealth and material possessions every several years to sponsor prayers and spiritual practice, and to provide for those in need. It's hard to imagine giving up everything we have even once in this lifetime, not to mention doing it every several years. These great masters knew that ordinary people struggle to give of themselves, so they took it upon themselves to demonstrate the great courage and strength of mind it takes to give up everything, hoping to inspire us to be willing to give up just a little.

▰▱▻ Although we may not be capable of willingly giving up everything at this time in our lives, reflect on this example of great courage, selflessness, and generosity, and aspire to follow in the footsteps of these great masters.

DAY 7

Generosity is the first of the *paramitas*, perfections or transcendental actions.

Ordinary giving is the cause for great merit and virtue. It supports our spiritual development and helps us to cut through our ego and attachment to this life. However, when we recognize the truly insubstantial nature of ourselves, the object we are giving, and the recipient of our generosity, only then does our act of giving rise from the ordinary to the level of a paramita. And as a result, the merit accumulated through our transcendental act of giving, no matter how large or small, will remain with us until we reach the state of complete enlightenment.

▰▱▻ As you work at giving throughout your daily life, mindfully recall the insubstantial and impermanent nature of yourself and of the world around you.

Day 8

We can begin to make other types of offerings on our altar to support our practice of generosity. Candles are another traditional daily offering that is customarily made in the Buddhist tradition; a candle flame is symbolic of dispelling the darkness of ignorance. By lighting the candles and dedicating the offering to all beings, we're not only training the mind in altruism, but we're also training in using our money for a sacred purpose rather than using it merely to fulfill our own desires.

▰▭▻ You can buy beautiful scented candles, or small crystal tea light holders and a box of tea lights, and begin to offer three candles on your altar each morning just after you offer water. Arrange the offerings beautifully, mindfully, and with a positive motivation. After you light the candles, think, "By this offering, may all beings everywhere be free of painful emotions, aggression, and ignorance, and may their minds be illuminated by wisdom."

Day 9

The second of the three types of generosity is called the "generosity of protecting others from fear."

There are all types of fear to be experienced in the world. Some are imposed by outer forces, such as a malevolent government or a civil war. Some are imposed by natural conditions, such as a lack of rain that leads to famine or an earthquake that leads to a tsunami or the demolition of an entire community. Yet even those of us who grow up in a stable democratic society that has abundant food and resources still feel intense fears such as the fear of being alone, the fear of vulnerability, the fear of being harmed, the fear of loss, and the fear of death.

In our daily lives, we have many chances to protect others from fear. For example, we can offer our money and resources to help refugees or those who have suffered in a natural disaster. We can offer love and support to others facing difficult times. We can offer emotional support to those facing death or set an example of fearlessness as we face the dying process, as a gift to those we leave behind.

▰▱▷ What can you do to lessen the energy of fear in the world?

DAY 10

Listening to others is a form of generosity.

We all know how it feels to talk to someone who only focuses the conversation on themselves and doesn't let us get a word in edgewise. We can feel frustrated by our inability to connect, participate, and share with the other person in these situations. However, instead of being frustrated, we could reframe this same experience as a chance for us to focus on another's needs and practice the art of giving. Rather than getting frustrated that we weren't listened to fairly and equally, we can simply focus on the other person, doing our best to offer them relief and comfort.

▰▱▷ Today, find a way to be generous enough to truly listen to the words of another.

DAY 11

Many of us feel that simplicity is the key to a happy life. This statement is true—but only if it's a simplicity that arises from the heart, not our surrounding environment.

We may feel that simplicity is an uncomplicated lifestyle that includes lack of money and expensive belongings, but this is a misunderstanding. There's nothing inherently spiritual about being poor. For example, how would living in a smaller house actually make us more loving and kind? Does having less money make us less selfish?

Loving and giving to others wholeheartedly and without the complications of attachment, anger, pride, or jealousy is the true essence of simplicity. This type of simplicity comes from within ourselves and is not dependent on any outer situation.

If we wish to die confidently, we should begin to question our own attitude toward simplicity.

▰▷ Today, try to connect to the simplicity that is a state of heart and mind.

DAY 12

In Tibet, there was a great master named Yukok Chattral. In the Tibetan language, the name Chattral means "possessionless." A yogi who is given the title of Chattral does not own anything. Such a yogi gives away everything he or she has.

One day, Lama Chupur, a great Dzogchen yogi from Amdo, went to see Yukok Chattral. But when he entered the yogi's room, he found that Yukok Chattral was surrounded by all kinds of beautiful ritual objects. Lama Chupur asked, "I thought you were a possessionless yogi."

Yukok Chattral replied, "I don't chase after possessions. Possessions chase after me."

It was a perfect answer to Lama Chupur's question. Even though Yukok Chattral had many beautiful things, through his spiritual mastery, he achieved true simplicity. Unlike normal people, who hoard all of the beautiful objects around them, Yukok Chattral gave away whatever he received—only to be showered again with abundance. His example shows that when we achieve genuine simplicity, we are truly free to give.

▰▷ Today, reflect on this story, which illustrates the nature of simplicity.

Day 13

One way to practice generosity is to give what we actually have. For example, we might send a check to sponsor Thanksgiving dinner at a homeless shelter or give a winter jacket to a clothing drive. We can share a pot of tea with a friend or give a gift to a loved one. There are endless ways in which we could share what we have with others.

Another form of generosity practice taught in the Vajrayana Buddhist tradition is to "offer the things enjoyed by others." This practice helps us to give up any grasping or coveting toward others' good fortune. We often have feelings of envy, or even judgment, toward a person who has something that we wish we had for ourselves—a nice car, a fashionable pair of shoes, a lucrative and prestigious job, an attractive partner or spouse. Instead of chasing after that feeling of envy, we can rejoice in the person's good fortune and wish that all other beings could enjoy the same thing. By rejoicing in the good things that others have, we can protect ourselves from greed toward the possessions of others, and bring ourselves happiness in the process. When we cut through envy and jealousy toward the good fortune of others, we are one step closer to dying free of all attachments.

▰▱▷ Today, rejoice in something possessed by another that you wish you had for yourself. For example, if you are longing for an intimate relationship and see a beautiful couple walking down the street, obviously in love, rejoice in their happiness rather than feeling envy or saddened by what you don't have.

Day 14

We should start to develop a generous motivation toward our paid employment, or toward whatever material wealth or possessions that we have. We may have had the idea that our job has to be life-changing, for either ourselves or others, in order to bring positive energy into the world. But money itself can be the currency of generous, positive energy. When we have money, we are free to support charitable causes such as medical research, a homeless shelter, a community garden, a scholarship program, a Dharma center, our spiritual friend, and a great many other projects and organizations that can better our community, the nation, and the world. Therefore, we should cultivate gratitude toward our employer or to whatever source of income we have for providing us with this opportunity.

Some of us may feel that we don't have enough financial resources to contribute to charitable causes, but in truth, we are all capable of sharing what we have. Even if we aren't wealthy, we can surely find a way to give something. We should take time to consider what good we could do with the amount of money we spend, for example, on a cup of coffee or eating a meal out. Could we give up a night out with friends and enjoy the evening at home instead, giving what we would have spent to a force for positive change in the world? It's perfectly fine to start with a small action. In the Dharma, we say that great results can ripen even from a small seed.

How can the money you have be used to support positive change?

DAY 15

Once we're comfortable with the idea of making offerings as a support for spiritual development, we may want to try making other kinds of offerings on our altar. We can offer anything symbolic or beautiful. Fruit can symbolize maturity and spiritual development. Flowers are an expression of beauty and also a reminder of impermanence. We can offer beautifully scented incense and color our offering water with saffron.

We may want to add other sources of inspiration to our altar as well. For example, we might wish to place a framed picture of a special deity such as Avalokiteshvara, who represents the perfect and undying expression of compassion for all sentient beings. Over time, we may feel more comfortable spending money on our altar and might be inspired to add other things to beautify our sacred space: a special cushion for sitting practice, a crystal pitcher to fill and empty our water bowls, an elegant flower made from delicate, blown glass. All of these things can help the mind to feel relaxed, at ease, and inspired when we sit down to reflect, pray, or meditate each day.

✏️ What can you add to your altar to encourage your mindfulness and connection to your spiritual practice?

DAY 16

We need not limit our practice of generosity to material possessions. Another way we can make offerings is to offer "things not possessed"— natural expressions of beauty in the world around us that delight us and make us feel happy to be alive: a meadow full of deer, a clear blue sky, crocuses blooming through the snow, a butterfly, stained glass tinged by the evening sun, the quiet calm of dawn, the fierce love of a puppy. Rather than clinging to any of these delightful sensory experiences, we can simply offer them from our own minds, wishing that all beings may share in the same enjoyment. In this way, our expression of generosity can become fuller and more complete: a wish that others share not only our material enjoyments but our comforts, happiness, and delights as well.

✏️ Today, be mindful of any special beautiful moments or experiences and offer them for all beings' enjoyment.

DAY 17

The third type of generosity is the "generosity of Dharma." Primarily, this refers to lamas who are qualified to teach the Dharma and help students develop their practice. However, there are many ways we can practice the generosity of the Dharma. We can become a monthly contributing member to a Dharma center and support ongoing teachings and programs at that center, and we can support our spiritual friend. We can show up for practice, set an example, and greet newcomers, helping them to feel welcome and at home in our center. We can take responsibility for programs, renovation, cleaning, or any of the other many tasks that need to be completed for a spiritual community to run smoothly. Of course, in our will, we also have the chance to donate a portion of our estate to ensure that Dharma remains firmly rooted for many generations to come.

Sometimes we have the feeling that our own efforts are too small to be of benefit to others. But when we combine our energy with others who are like-minded, our efforts can bring remarkable results.

▰▷ What are you currently doing to give the gift of Dharma? What more could you do?

Day 18

We can view the effort we put into preparing for death as an act of generosity that benefits both ourselves and others. When we're willing to commit to a life-long spiritual practice, we are able to give others the gift of our own spiritual preparation and growth. We do so both by setting an example and also by tearing down our own walls and being willing to be present for others in a very painful world. When we're willing to be present for the experiences of aging, sickness, and our own mortality, we also give others permission to do the same.

▰▷ Today, challenge yourself to see your own spiritual progress as a gift to others.

DAY 19

We should all sit down to draft our Dharma Will: a document stating our wishes for spiritual care as we are dying and after our death. It's also our last opportunity to do good in this world.

Our Dharma Will will outlive us, and the instructions we place within it will be carried out by our entrusted Dharma friends after we have left this body behind. We should reflect on how we could use the wealth we have accumulated during this lifetime in the most positive manner. Of course, we should provide for our loved ones who depend on us, but we can also find ways to support organizations that work for the welfare of others and to repay the kindnesses that others have shown us. We may want to imagine how we could create the same meaningful or life-changing opportunities that we have had for others. For example, if we have suffered from an illness, we may wish to support a hospice that cared for us or a research hospital. If our education was sponsored, we may wish to dedicate funds to a school or for a scholarship. If we have been cared for by a spiritual community and a spiritual friend, we may wish to offer financial support to that organization to help the group continue its mission.

▣▷ What's in your Dharma Will? Will it help you achieve your aspirations to benefit others? How can you best serve others through the experience of dying?

DAY 20

It is important that we prepare now for the day that our Dharma Will is carried out. Our Dharma Will should be a bold plan, a beautiful aspiration of how the entirety of everything we have accumulated during our lives can be used to bring happiness to others. We should try to enjoy making the plan, savoring the feeling of our generous aspiration. But then we should also realize that simply making this aspiration and writing it down is not enough. After all, when we are in the *bardo* state, the states beyond death before we take rebirth, we will actually see our possessions and our money being given away, and we may feel distraught that we are being left with nothing.

As we draft our Dharma Will, we should become aware of any hesitancy we have to part with our possessions. We should note where our strong attachments are. When we notice ourselves wanting to cling to something we know that we cannot possess indefinitely, we should mindfully reflect on the impermanent and changeable nature of all phenomena.

➡ What possessions might be difficult for you to give up? Reflect on your attachment to your possessions.

DAY 21

At the time of death, we will have to give up even this precious body, which we hold dearer than any of our possessions. Many aspiration prayers in the Vajrayana Buddhist tradition speak to the difficulty of this act; when we recite them, we train in the willingness to let go of our current physical guesthouse—especially if it can benefit another being directly. Such practices help us prepare for the shock of having to part with our constant companion, the physical body.

We may wish to visualize our own body as a corpse and gaze down upon it as though we are viewing it from above. Some of us may wish to become organ or tissue donors once death is imminent. To this end, we should train continuously in bodhichitta and in the aspiration that we will be able to offer our body to save another person's life free from any attachment toward ourselves. We may even wish to give away a part of our physical body now to help us train in the act of giving away our physical body, such as by donating blood.

➡ Begin to see your body as being in a state of perpetual decay, something that can be given up at a moment's notice.

Day 22

One way to test how far our generosity practice has come is to try to give something we want for ourselves to someone else. Depending on where we are in our training, we can do this in a variety of ways. We might start with something simple. While having dinner with friends or loved ones, we can notice what we most want to take for ourselves. Then, we can deliberately choose not to take it and offer it to someone else instead, rejoicing in their enjoyment. If we feel our generosity practice is getting stronger, we might want to buy something we want for ourselves and give it to someone else as a gift. We can also challenge ourselves to give away a cherished or prized possession to someone else who may enjoy it.

Where can you begin to work on giving something you want for yourself? Choose something and give it a try.

Day 23

In the Tibetan Buddhist tradition, we make a symbolic offering called "offering the mandala." *Mandala* is a Sanskrit word that refers to our entire phenomenal universe in its perfect state. We use a ritual mandala plate and recite a prayer while we fill it with precious stones and place it on our altar.

It's possible to misunderstand a practice like offering the mandala, thinking it's just an empty ritual. However, when done with the proper motivation, offering the mandala helps to bring an expansive and generous quality to the mind; we offer everything we have, as well as all things in the entire phenomenal universe, for the benefit of all beings to reach perfect enlightenment.

Offering the mandala embodies the true spirit of dying with confidence. If we can develop such confidence in offering all that we have during our ordinary life, we will carry this confidence with us to the moment of death.

▰▭▷ Today, make a mental offering of everything you have and the whole phenomenal world as well as a support for the enlightenment and happiness of all sentient beings. If you have a mandala set, offer it and place it on your altar.

DAY 24

When a loved one is in pain or dying, we may choose to offer them support in the form of our love, our prayers, and the commitment to carry out their wishes. Also, we may have made the more formal commitment to become an entrusted Dharma friend to this person. If we have, we should do everything we can to show up in their hour of need. Sometimes people feel that it's too difficult to rearrange their schedules and show up at the hospital or on a friend's deathbed on a moment's notice. They ask, "Can't I just pray for my loved one from where I am? Why won't that be effective?"

In these situations, we should always reflect on how we would feel if the positions were reversed. If we were the one dying, it would be so meaningful to us that our entrusted Dharma friends made the effort and sacrifice to be with us during that all-important time. We should not fool ourselves into thinking the gift of our presence isn't important and that we have more pressing things to do.

▰▭▷ Today, remember that although we live our lives every day, the moment of death will only come once.

DAY 25

In addition to offering our own prayers and service toward a loved one who is dying, we may also wish to make donations to a Buddhist monastery, a spiritual master, or an organization like the Phowa Foundation to have prayers or *phowa*, transfer of consciousness practices, done to benefit our loved one at the time of death.

Many of us resist the idea of making a donation when prayers are requested; we wonder what the purpose of the donation is. Of course, there is the ordinary reason that spiritual endeavors have always been supported by the generosity of the community, and that such organizations cannot exist without the support of laypeople. But in the Vajrayana tradition, the reason is actually much more meaningful.

It is said that a great master cannot benefit a being with whom he or she has no karmic connection. A karmic connection can be anything; it can be either positive or negative, but the two beings must somehow be connected. Without the proper energetic connection, even a great *siddha*, a realized being, cannot benefit the dying. By offering something, whether money or even a meaningful possession, we forge a karmic connection between the master and the deceased.

Of course, we are rewarded well for our generosity. We receive the benefit of training in selfless generosity: giving solely for another's benefit and well-being, and dedicating our action and effort to them.

✏️ Today, research spiritual organizations that you could donate to when the occasion arises. Can you start today?

DAY 26

Patrul Rinpoche was a miraculous siddha who lived in Tibet in the 1800s. Although he was a completely realized master, he didn't look the part. He wandered here and there, dressed like a wandering beggar.

One day he ended up at the house of a wealthy family whose son had just died. They had invited a well-known lama to come and practice phowa. The lama and his attendant were given food and gifts when they arrived. Patrul Rinpoche was given nothing, but he joined the others and all three lamas began to offer prayers.

As the well-known lama offered his prayers, his mind wandered to what he would receive in return for his service, so his motivation to benefit the deceased was corrupted. The lama's attendant had a deep and pure wish to benefit the deceased, but he had no training and didn't know how to perform phowa. Patrul Rinpoche both wished to benefit the deceased and had the ability to do so, but because the family had given him nothing, he had no connection to the deceased. He held out his bowl and begged for a drink of sour buttermilk. After the buttermilk was given, he was able to practice phowa and bring the deceased to a highly realized state.

As the story shows, karmic connection is everything. What we give matters less than the act of giving itself.

☞ Reflect on this story about the great master Patrul Rinpoche, which shows that it doesn't matter if you don't have very much to give.

DAY 27

It's important to plan for our own death in detail. Have we thought of saving money to sponsor our lama to be at our bedside, if possible, or to practice phowa for us? Do we wish to have the customary forty-nine days of prayers done for us in accordance with the Tibetan Buddhist tradition? If we would like these types of support during the dying process, we had better start planning. After all, it's unlikely that a friend or family member will sponsor these activities for us.

☞ After you envision what you would like to happen during and after your death, you should incorporate these details into your Dharma Will and then entrust one of your Dharma friends to complete all of the necessary arrangements.

Day 28

Generosity is the first of the paramitas because it is the foundation for all the others. Generosity brings us willingness: willingness to change, to give up what we want for another, to be satisfied with what we have, to be flexible, to compromise, to cherish others more than ourselves. Generosity brings us a vast and open mind that has enough room for everyone and everything. The great Indian master Chandrakirti said, "The cause for easing suffering arises from the practice of generosity."

▣▷ Reflect on the ways in which generosity can help you develop other good qualities, such as compassion, loving-kindness, and fearlessness.

Day 29

▣▷ Do something generous for a stranger today. Pay for their coffee. Let a car merge in front of you when you are in a hurry. Say something kind, comforting, or reassuring. Challenge yourself.

Day 30

▣▷ Take a few moments to rejoice in the effort you made during the past month. Dedicate any good that came from your contemplative practice for the benefit of all sentient beings.

Developing a Daily Practice

A N INTEGRAL PART of dying confidently is having an unshakable daily practice. "Unshakable" means that we practice no matter what kind of difficult situation we are facing, no matter how upset we are or what obstacles there may be—as Anyen Rinpoche says: even if the sky is falling. Surely, at the moment of death, we will also face a rush of difficult emotions and fears. We have no idea what kind of situation will be the cause of our death—whether it will be preceded by illness, an accident, or violent circumstances. If our practice is not unshakable during our daily life, how can we ever imagine we'll be able to practice in the face of death?

Now, as we enter the tenth month of our year-long commitment, it's time for us to evaluate our daily practice as it has developed thus far. Where we find strengths, we'll improve on them. Where we find weakness and lacking, we will send in reinforcements and new structures. There is hard work for us ahead, but if we face it with enthusiasm and joy, we're sure to find the unshakable result we are seeking.

DAY 1

Wake up! Death may arrive at any moment.

➡️ Have you practiced yet today? Did you skip practice, or give it less energy, thinking that you will have time to catch up later? Did you give practice your utmost attention today?

DAY 2

It's important to periodically examine our normal practice routine.

➡️ Review the notes in your journal about your daily practice. Do you practice at the same time each day? Are you committed to a certain practice, or have you been working with this book as a daily practice?

In the last ten months, how many times have you skipped practice? Did you engage in each daily contemplation so far?

DAY 3

➡️ Stop whatever you're doing right now and make an aspiration prayer for your own daily practice and spiritual development, and for the ability to fearlessly face the moment of death. If you like, you can use a lineage prayer such as *Entering the City of Omniscience* by Jigme Lingpa, or you can reflect on the first chapter of Shantideva's *Guide to the Bodhisattva's Way of Life*. Or you can simply make an auspicious wish that you will have the capacity to be a great spiritual practitioner, who has an unshakable mind and unshakable practice, who is able to benefit all beings to whom you are connected.

Try to kindle a feeling of warmth in your heart, and send that wish to benefit all sentient beings out from your heart center.

Day 4

Daily practice must be supported by an ironclad commitment.

▣▷ Today, make a commitment for daily practice that you will keep for the next thirty days—no matter what. Pick a length of practice time that you are sure you can work with each day as a start. We'll check in over the next thirty days and see if an increase in practice time is appropriate.

Take a moment to write down any details about your practice commitment. Tape a copy of it somewhere you'll see it on a daily basis to remind yourself: the bathroom mirror, the refrigerator, or on the nightstand beside your bed.

Day 5

During our thirty-day practice commitment, we will work on four types of close examination. This type of work helps us notice whether either we ourselves or outer phenomenon have any lasting or permanent qualities.

The first one we'll work with is a close examination of the body. Over the next several days, we'll add aspects of this examination to our daily practice.

▣▷ Today, contemplate why you are attached to your body. What causes you to make it look beautiful? What causes your resistance to aging?

Day 6

What is the essence of our bodies? We have all contemplated impermanence thoroughly. We know that our own bodies, like all other phenomena, are made up of constituent parts like flesh, blood, nerves, bones, and organs.

▄▄▶ Do you still feel that your body has a real essence that you can grasp and hold on to? If so, why?

DAY 7

If the body has no essence, where can we find the "self"?

▄▄▶ Take some time to scan the different parts and components of your body. Can the self be found in any of them? Examine your flesh, blood, skin, bones, and organs. Start at the top of your head and move all the way down to the tips of your toes.

Can your "self" be found anywhere? Why are you so attached to the idea that the body is "yourself"?

DAY 8

The Dharma Box is a special box in which we place all of the things that we would like to have with us during the dying process. For example, we might place within it photographs of our lama or special images that we would like placed on a bedside altar in the event of a serious, life-threatening illness. We might also want to place copies of any prayers or practices that we do on a daily basis so they can be read to us while we are dying.

▄▄▶ Have you begun to assemble your Dharma Box? What other supports would you like to have with you at the time of death?

DAY 9

Most of us already set up an altar to support our practice earlier this year. However, at this point, we should take a second look at the things we have chosen as supports for our practice.

Were any of them purchased with a motivation of greed? For example, did we buy candleholders, offering bowls, or a table that were cheaply made—even if we could afford better—because we didn't want to spend money on them? Or do we notice how interacting with our altar each day, by offering water, candles, fruit, or flowers, increases our sense of ritual and commitment to our practice time?

▰▱▻ What's on your altar? How do the objects support or impede your practice?

DAY 10

A week has passed since we made our formal thirty-day practice commitment; it's time to check in with how it has gone so far.

▰▱▻ Have you had any difficulty keeping your commitment? What kinds of things have distracted you or made you feel you didn't have time to practice?

DAY 11

Another part of committing to practice is showing up for scheduled practices and supporting the activities of the spiritual community.

▰▱▻ Do you belong to a Dharma center or have a formal place you go to practice? This month, make a strong commitment not to miss any scheduled practice sessions at your Dharma center.

Are there special skills or talents you have that might benefit the lama, the center, or the community? Can you offer some of your personal time to the community this month?

DAY 12

Today, we'll begin the second of the four types of examination: close examination of our feelings and emotions.

✏️ Do you identify more with your body or with your emotions? In what way do your attachments to your body and feelings overlap? Are your feelings "you"?

DAY 13

We're now ten days into our formal thirty-day practice commitment; it's time to check in with our practice and see if an increase in practice time is appropriate.

✏️ Can you increase your commitment by five or ten minutes each day, still feeling comfortable that you will complete the thirty days without skipping any sessions? How about by two minutes?

DAY 14

Today we'll continue our close examination of the emotions and our attachment to them.

Even the English language shows our cultural identification with the emotions. We say "I am angry" rather than putting any space between the emotion and ourselves. The Tibetan language expresses the same idea as "anger is there."

▬▷ Do you notice having attachment to your emotions, or do your emotions just seem part of "you"? Which emotions do you seem to act out the most? For example, do you tend to be a person who is angry, jealous, funny, or intense?

DAY 15

▬▷ Today, engage in an exercise in mindfulness and introspection. Put a handful of dry beans in your left pant or jacket pocket (this may require some thought when you choose your outfit today). During the day, each time you notice yourself identifying with an emotion, move a bean from your left pocket to your right.

At the end of the day, how many times did you notice yourself identify with your emotions? Was it more or less than you thought?

DAY 16

▬▷ Today, again engage in the mindfulness and introspection exercise. At the end of the day, evaluate the difference between yesterday and today. Did you notice yourself identifying with your emotions more today than yesterday? Did your ability to notice your emotional state improve today?

DAY 17

▬▷ Today, once more engage in the mindfulness and introspection exercise. At the end of the day, again evaluate the difference between yesterday and today. Did you notice yourself identifying with your emotions more today than yesterday? Did your ability to notice your emotional state improve today? How about in relation to the first day?

DAY 18

Feelings include those of the mind and those of the body. Feelings constantly arise in body and mind one after another.

What will the experience of death be like if we are attached to our feelings?

▰▷ If we identify with our feelings, will we have any opportunity to practice when we are dying? Will we remember our spiritual practice?

DAY 19

No matter how "real" our body or feelings seem right now, they are bound to change.

▰▷ Today, as part of your close examination, reflect on the lack of inherent existence of body and mind. Take a moment to notice the strongest sensation or feeling you have right now. Reevaluate it throughout the day.

How do you notice that it has changed? Even seeing that it has changed, do you feel it is impermanent?

DAY 20

Now we'll engage in the third examination: close examination of the conceptual mind, the mind that puts words and labels to our thoughts and emotions, as well as the environment around us.

▦➤ Notice how conceptual thoughts relate to emotions. Do your thoughts seem to arise simultaneously with your emotions, or one after another?

DAY 21

▦➤ During your sitting practice, try the following exercise: Take out a handful of beans and place them on the floor beside you. Each time you notice a conceptual thought arise during your practice, move one of the beans and make a new pile.

At the end of your practice period, how many conceptual thoughts did you count? Are you surprised to see how much you think while you meditate?

DAY 22

▦➤ Continue your close examination of conceptual thoughts. Today, while sitting on the cushion, try to notice the pattern of your thoughts.

Do they seem to have a related theme? What emotional tendency seems to be expressed by your conceptual thoughts? What weakness does the pattern of your thoughts show?

Day 23

➤ Having noticed the emotional qualities of your conceptual thoughts, is it possible for you to work at transforming them today?

For example, if you have pervasively angry thoughts, can you work at applying bodhichitta or use any of the techniques you have learned so far to turn the energy of your conceptual thoughts around? What difficulties do you encounter when you attempt to do so?

Day 24

➤ Check in with your Dharma Vision and your formal practice commitment. Is the commitment you made going to be enough to carry you toward the vision you have for your practice at the time of death? If not, make aspiration prayers that you will be willing to dedicate yourself to the hard work it'll take to achieve that vision while you are still healthy and alive, and that you are willing to do so for the benefit of all sentient beings.

Day 25

We're about twenty days into our thirty-day commitment, so it's time to check in with our daily practice.

➤ How is your practice going? Would it be appropriate to increase your practice session by five or ten minutes and still complete the commitment? Are any other changes needed?

DAY 26

Today we'll begin the final of the four examinations: close examination of all phenomena in the material world.

▣▷ What material thing are you most attached to? Why? Are you surprised to discover what it is?

DAY 27

In order to die confidently, we'll have to be willing to give up all attachment to ourselves and outer phenomena in a single moment.

▣▷ Today, reflect on the thing you're most attached to. Using this one thing as a metaphor for all of the other attachments in your life, make aspiration prayers to become willing to give up everything you have and dedicate yourself solely to spiritual practice for the benefit of all sentient beings.

DAY 28

Family and love relationships are an aspect of the material world to which we are extremely attached. When we were determining the thing we're most attached to, did we remember to consider the relationships we have with our parents, our spouse, and our children?

▣▷ How difficult is it to imagine giving that relationship up in a single instant? When you contemplate in this manner, does it change your impression of how difficult it will be to practice at the moment of death?

DAY 29

When we make a formal aspiration to give away what we have, we grapple with and attempt to sever the attachments that live within the mind. If we do our best to give in support of our loved ones, our spiritual friend, our spiritual center, and causes we care about, we have no need to reflect on those attachments at the time of death. We will find the mind is clear and open, ready to engage in the next experience.

▄▭▷ Take some time to update your Dharma Will. Reflect on how giving away what you have will support your practice at the moment of death.

DAY 30

▄▭▷ Take a few moments to rejoice in the effort you made during the past month. Dedicate any good that came from your contemplative practice for the benefit of all sentient beings.

Cultivating Patience

PATIENCE IS A QUALITY that we must master in order to die confidently.

From the moment we took birth until now, and from this moment forward until we actually face the moment of death, our lives will be filled with disappointment and suffering. We will face unwanted situations that we have no choice but to accept. We will have to live with difficulties that we tried to deny and bent over backward trying to avoid. And we will have to find a way to smile and have the willingness to keep practicing even when we feel we are not capable of taking even another moment of pain.

How will we face all of these difficulties in life without patience? Without it, we will not progress on the spiritual path; our lack of patience will rob us of any possible opportunity to practice. When everything else we think we can depend on falls apart, patience will be the only thing left to help us pick up the pieces. It is the only thing that can give us the energy and the presence of mind to continue practicing.

Patience must be our constant companion. When we face the experience of dying, that moment when we're about to lose everything we have held dear, how else will we manage to have a stable, compassionate, and confident state of mind? Knowing this, we should work diligently at developing patience over the next thirty days.

DAY 1

▣▷ Do you think of yourself as a patient person? What triggers impatience in you?

Today, take a few moments to journal about how you see your current capacity to practice patience.

DAY 2

Patience toward oneself can be a great support for practice. We may feel we are not good enough to become a genuine practitioner of the Dharma. We may feel that we lack positive qualities or that others are more deserving or better than us. When these kinds of feelings arise, practicing patience toward ourselves can enable us to work through these kinds of self-destructive feelings and motivate ourselves to keep practicing.

▣▷ Today, reflect on your attitude toward yourself and your practice. Do you have a healthy, patient view of yourself?

DAY 3

Patience toward oneself can also be a great obstacle to practice. We may not want to give up our own way of doing things, feeling that our way is the best. We may make mistakes and brush them aside too easily, not taking time to properly regret our own actions and make a commitment to change. We may feel critical of others and tolerant of ourselves. Practicing patience in a selfish manner will degrade our spiritual practice.

▣▷ Today, discern if there are ways you practice patience in a way that is unhealthy.

Day 4

▰▷ Are you patient toward others? Do you find it easy to reflect on others' feelings and the situations they are facing? Is your practice of patience genuine, or do you pretend to be patient but harbor resentment on the inside?

Today, investigate the quality of patience you feel in relation to others.

Day 5

The great master Shantideva said, "There is no emotion more destructive than anger, and no quality more difficult to master than patience."

▰▷ Reflect on this quotation. Consider copying Shantideva's words and placing them somewhere you will see them often.

Day 6

We are often deeply confused when we hear teachings about patience. We may think that when masters tell us to be patient we are being told to be apathetic, and consequently we may sink unhappily into a negative situation. We may think that when we are told to be content we should avoid making changes in our lives. Both of these ways of thinking are false choices presented by the ego, which is trying desperately to maintain its status as the ruler of our world. Patience is a sense of inner peace. It is the dense, stable energy within the mind that allows us the ability to reflect and make thoughtful decisions and to act instead of react.

▰▷ Do you have any confusion or uncertainty regarding patience?

Day 7

▰▷ Tonight, take some time before you go to sleep to reflect on and write down moments in which you experienced impatience during the day. Think of different kinds of situations where you lost your peace of mind. Some of them may have occurred during conversations with others, when you were engaging in ordinary activities like driving or buying a cup of coffee, or even without any seeming provocation—simply based on a memory of something from the past.

Day 8

All of the suffering we feel in life actually arises from impatience, the quality of being unwilling to accept a particular experience or situation. Because the mind wishes to avoid the experience, we suffer when we are forced to go through it.

▰▷ Have you had a personal experience like this? Do you believe your own impatient attitude exacerbated the negativity of it?

Day 9

So many situations we face will bring us suffering if we cannot develop patience. Each and every day, for instance, we face change. If we cannot tolerate it, we are sure to experience great suffering.

▰▷ Think of an example of change that you noticed today. It could be something as minor as someone treating you differently than you expected or a longer-than-usual commute.

What was your experience of that change? Did you apply patience?

Day 10

▨⇨ Today, commit to practice patience with a chosen person or situation. It could be while shopping at the grocery store, having a conversation with your mother, or visiting with a coworker.

Did your commitment to practice patience affect your ability to actually do it? Or did you get impatient in spite of your commitment?

Day 11

The four rivers of birth, old age, sickness, and death can all be faced with the armor of patience.

▨⇨ Reflect again on the inevitability of aging, sickness, and death, that these four rivers will carry you through all the stages of life and death. Does this reflection increase your willingness to develop patience?

Day 12

▨⇨ Today, deliberately choose to do something that you know causes you to feel impatient. For example, if you normally avoid going shopping by ordering a certain product online, today go to the store and buy it. Or if you avoid talking to a certain person at work, today make a point to greet them and ask them how they are doing. Challenge yourself.

Day 13

One method for practicing patience is to reflect on the nature of karma.

▣➤ When you find yourself facing something unwanted, think to yourself, "Based on our positive and negative actions, we accumulate karma that is sure to ripen in the future. At this very moment, any situation I'm facing is an expression of karma accumulated in the past. Once it has ripened, that karma will no longer be with me."

Day 14

Being carried by the river of aging causes us much suffering. How do we cultivate patience with the often-unwanted experience of aging?

▣➤ Today, think of how aging is something you have in common with everyone and everything. Reflect on how all beings in the world are aging. All plants, animals, and even inanimate phenomena like rocks, pavement, and cement are aging.

Day 15

When we refuse to accept things we have no control over, we intensify our own experience of suffering.

▣➤ How does your resistance to aging make you feel tired, stressed out, or inadequate?

Day 16

▣➤ Today, again deliberately choose to do something you know causes you to feel impatient. If you hate driving in traffic, venture out at rush hour. If you dislike a particular political point of view, listen to a talk radio show that discusses the virtues of that point of view. Explore what it's like to practice patience in a provocative circumstance.

DAY 17

Being carried by the river of sickness also causes us deep and profound suffering.

▶ Today, reflect on the pain caused by an ordinary imbalance, like a headache. If you're unable to be patient when you have a headache, how will you ever deal with the suffering caused by a serious illness like cancer?

DAY 18

▶ Do some research on a few types of serious illnesses. Look at how many people around the world suffer each year from cancer, heart disease, or diabetes. Do you feel that sickness is inevitable? How will you deal with sickness when it comes for you?

DAY 19

Being carried by the river of death also causes us deep and profound suffering.

▶ Investigate plagues that have killed vast numbers of people in the history of the world, such as smallpox, the Spanish flu, or the black plague. Look at modern epidemics like malaria and AIDS. Do you feel that death is inevitable? How will you deal with death when it comes for you?

DAY 20

One method for practicing patience is to reflect on the nature of samsara: suffering that cannot be escaped. When we accept the reality of life as it is, we are more likely to practice and find a way to work with a situation rather than focusing on finding an escape or a way to fix it.

▣▷ When you face a painful or unwanted situation today, reflect on the fact that lasting happiness is an unattainable fantasy.

DAY 21

Often the result of not practicing patience is worse than what would happen if we were patient. For example, if we feel angry with a friend, we could choose to either practice patience or to retaliate. If we practice patience, we will have some feelings of discomfort to deal with, and we will also have to make effort at some kind of antidote to help us work through the negative emotions we feel. But if we retaliate, we may cause damage to the relationship. We will likely express our anger and have to deal with the negative feelings that arise then. We will probably have to deal with a heated discussion or an argument that cannot be immediately resolved.

▣▷ Reflect on how this type of complicated result could have been avoided if you'd been willing to practice patience and let it go.

DAY 22

▣▷ Today, once again, deliberately choose to do something you know causes you to feel impatient. Put on a wool sweater that makes you itch. Draw a cold bath and get in, seeing if you can bear the feeling of cold on your skin.

DAY 23

Another method for dealing with difficult situations is reflecting on the phrase "Why *wouldn't* it happen to me?" Usually, when we face difficulties, we wonder what we have done to bring us to such a painful situation. However, we can turn this way of thinking on its head and instead try to realize that all beings living in samsara are constantly facing unwanted situations. So why wouldn't we also face unwanted and painful circumstances?

▧➤ Notice any times in your day when you find yourself thinking, "Why me?" Remind yourself that such situations happen to everyone and are an unavoidable aspect of life, thinking instead, "Why *wouldn't* it happen to me?"

DAY 24

If we're lucky enough to be conscious and aware at the moment of death, that is the moment where patience will benefit us the most. During this instant, we will face the most unwanted situation of our lives: the moment when we have to give up the body and life we cherish, and everything to which we are attached.

▧➤ Reflect on how profound your patience practice will have to be to benefit you at that moment. Try to increase your own motivation to practice.

DAY 25

Being unwilling to cultivate patience has many unhappy consequences. One is a mind filled with jealousy or competitiveness. If we are unwilling to tolerate the fact that others are enjoying the things we want for ourselves, we will experience deep unhappiness.

■➡ Today, reflect on a person who is enjoying something you wish you had. Can you rejoice in their happiness as a form of patience?

DAY 26

Impatient people suffer the most. Recall the "suffering of suffering" from month 5. If an unwanted situation arises, and on top of that we are impatient with that suffering, we intensify our own experience of pain.

■➡ Think of a time that you were suffering and caused yourself to suffer more. Did you recognize that you had the ability to decrease your own suffering by letting go of your own expectations?

DAY 27

The inability to accept the nature of karma causes us to blame ourselves or others for unwanted situations.

If we lack a patient attitude toward the difficulties we face in our lives, not realizing they are all an expression of previously accumulated karma, we'll look for someone to blame for our pain or discomfort. We may place the blame inside, upon ourselves, or outside, on someone else. Either way, we're sure to experience the suffering of suffering; we'll have even more discomfort as a result of blaming.

■➡ Do you have a tendency to blame rather than practice patience? How does blaming yourself or another affect your state of mind?

DAY 28

Part of patience is being with experiences, including sensory experiences, we find aversive. After all, sickness, aging, and the process of dying will inevitably include such things. Cultivating patience gives us a more carefree attitude, where we are less bothered by things we ordinarily find distasteful or annoying.

✏️ Today, engage your senses in a way that causes you to feel impatient. Turn on the fire alarm in your living room and listen to the sound for a few moments. Put salt on your tongue. Bite into a grapefruit rind and taste the bitter flavor. Sit down to meditate but leave the television blaring in the other room. Challenge yourself to bear a sensory experience that you would rather avoid.

DAY 29

✏️ Review your Dharma Vision and see which of your aspirations require patience. How much of your spiritual practice is related to patience?

DAY 30

✏️ Today, make aspiration prayers to give up the habit of blaming others for your own suffering, recognizing that any and all suffering can be diminished by the application of patience.

Day 31

▣▷ Take a few moments to rejoice in the effort you made during the past month. Dedicate any good that came from your contemplative practice for the benefit of all sentient beings.

Dedicating Ourselves for Others

IF WE DON'T dedicate ourselves for the benefit of others, we will never truly achieve confidence in the moment of death.

It is only through this dedication that we forget about ourselves and find happiness in the process. When we dedicate ourselves for the benefit of others, we turn our idea of loss upside down. By giving up ourselves, we gain enlightened qualities and lasting happiness. By holding on to what we think we have, and what we believe we need to survive, we constantly experience loss.

In order to dedicate ourselves for the benefit of others, we will need to gather together all of the skills that we have worked on developing this year. By understanding, practicing, and internalizing the essence of them all, we are sure to develop into practitioners who can die confidently. This month, as we again contemplate familiar ideas, we should challenge ourselves to deepen our own understanding and express the meaning of each of the spiritual principles in which we trained in a more authentic manner.

DAY 1

✐ Think back to yourself a year ago. How invested are you in avoiding the reality of unwanted circumstances, suffering, and death? Do you keep yourself as busy as you used to? What changes have you made for the better? Have you made any changes for the worse? What has stayed mostly the same?

DAY 2

Benefitting others takes many guises: Giving a friend or even a stranger a smile or a kind word. Offering emotional support to or expressing confidence in another when they're feeling down. Taking on the hardest part of a project at work to save someone else from having to do it. Dropping off dinner for a friend when they're busy.

▰▱▷ Today, notice all of the opportunities you have to benefit others. Challenge yourself to do something thoughtful for another. Notice how it makes you feel.

DAY 3

Joining a spiritual community gives us myriad opportunities to serve others. When we walk into the shrine room at our Dharma center, do we see anyone who looks unfamiliar or unsure of what is happening? Can we take personal responsibility for them, ensuring they feel comfortable and have the best possible experience?

▰▱▷ Challenge yourself to get out of your own shell and approach someone who seems to be struggling.

DAY 4

Each person who dies has their own story, just like we do. Like us, their lives are filled with things they do not want to leave behind—a spouse, children, extended family members, friends, their home, wealth, and possessions.

▰▻ Reflect on your thoughts and feelings from a year ago. Do you now feel more connected to the shared destiny of all sentient beings? How does this connection affect your state of mind? What would it mean to connect to this in an ongoing way?

DAY 5

Entering the Buddhist path is like committing to a life-long research project in which we investigate our own thoughts, habits, and reactions, and what makes us shut down. After all, if we're cultivating the heroic mind of a bodhisattva, nothing is off limits. We will have to face and work through every single difficulty that comes to us in life. Although rewarding, this can be a lonely journey.

▰▻ Think of yourself a year ago, and examine your commitment to the spiritual path and to benefitting others. Has your commitment increased? How have you faced the difficulties that have arisen over the past year? Where have you grown? What weaknesses remain? How would you like to approach the coming year's challenges?

DAY 6

All spiritual practice starts with an excellent motivation, which can help us bring joy and positive energy into any situation. No matter what feelings we may have about what is happening, our positive motivation can carry us beyond those personal emotions and connect with our greater spiritual intentions.

▧➤ Reflect on your mind as it is now, after a year of serious contemplative training. Has your motivation changed? Do you notice that you're kinder and more patient to others? Are you becoming less selfish and self-centered? Where in your life can you continue to work?

Day 7

Helping others is the key to happiness because by helping others we indirectly help ourselves. In Western culture, we are taught to balance our needs with the needs of others, but the Buddhist idea of transformation is much more revolutionary. The happiest person is the one who doesn't worry about him- or herself at all but is perfectly content based on concern for others.

▧➤ After your contemplative work this year, do you believe that helping others is a wish-fulfilling gem? Or do you still resist the idea that helping others can ultimately make you happy? Where does the resistance come from?

Day 8

▧➤ Today, challenge yourself to choose an activity that is truly for the benefit of others. For example, buy a sandwich for someone living on the street. Volunteer at a food bank. Call your parents and see what help you can offer them. Donate money to the first person who approaches you. If you can't carry out the activity today, plan what you will do and be sure to do it later this month.

DAY 9

▣▷ Over the next several days, take time to review the entries written in your journal over this past year.

Are you surprised by what you wrote? Do you see evidence of impermanence in your thoughts as recorded then, and what do you think now?

DAY 10

Ordinarily, our thoughts of impermanence are tied to change and loss, and having to accept the difficult truths of life. But impermanence also offers us the possibility of change for the better.

▣▷ Today, when you reflect on who you were a year ago, can you feel a sense of joy in the impermanence of your own spiritual journey?

DAY 11

One of the greatest supports we could have during the dying process would be to be with those to whom we have spiritually connected.

We have no idea when or where we will die, and we don't know if our spiritual friend will be present. Having several Dharma brothers and sisters we trust will make it more likely someone will be present for us.

▣▷ Have we made the effort to find entrusted Dharma brothers and sisters over this past year? Have we taken the opportunity to be of service to them when we can?

DAY 12

If we value the supportive conditions we have in our lives right now, the best way to ensure that they will continue is to share what we have with others. When we give away what we have and what we cherish most for others' happiness, we plant seeds for good fortune to come our way in the future. That is why one of the best ways to value our precious human life is to practice generosity—giving of our wealth, our time, and our energy.

➥ Reflect on the things that you value most in life. Do you feel joy in sharing them with others? Do you wish for others to take the same joy in them as you? Have you begun to give the things you cherish most?

DAY 13

➥ Today, open the draft you made of your Dharma Vision. Make additions, revisions, and changes as needed. Continue this process for several days if necessary.

DAY 14

➥ How does reflecting on the sufferings of ordinary life help you to dedicate your time, energy, and spiritual practice for the benefit of others? When you have less expectations of personal happiness, do you feel freer to focus on the well-being of those around you?

DAY 15

Ordinary life can be the source of much suffering.

▭▷ Challenge yourself to see everything you do as bodhisattva activity. For example, whether you're a waitress, a massage therapist, or a computer systems analyst, dedicate your entire profession and your personal effort to ease others' suffering. Think how you can use the fruits of your labor to benefit others directly or indirectly.

DAY 16

If we're mindful, we can use our gestures, demeanor, and energy to bring happiness to others, rather than upsetting them or making them uncomfortable. If we're mindful with our speech, we can use words to bring a feeling of peace and comfort to others, rather than speaking in a way that causes hurt or negative feelings. If we watch our own minds, we can start to notice our own negative thought patterns, and reduce their expression.

▭▷ How has your mindfulness improved over this year? Do you see your body, speech, and mind as a vehicle to bring constant happiness and benefit to others?

DAY 17

We may not be accustomed to thinking long and hard before we make a commitment. We may promise something as a social nicety or because we don't take it that seriously; we feel we can back out of the commitment if we need to. We may think that the promise we're making isn't that important and breaking it doesn't have the potential to hurt someone. However, when we fail to keep our commitments in worldly life, we will also fail to keep them in our spiritual life. How will we gain the potential to die confidently if we're not able to keep our commitments to daily practice, our spiritual friend, and our entrusted Dharma friends?

▣▷ How has our level of commitment changed to spiritual practice, our spiritual friend, and those who are our companions on the path? Do we see our commitment as part of dedicating ourselves for their benefit?

DAY 18

Keeping commitments can be a skillful way to learn to put others before ourselves. If we commit to something that we later regret, we might consider following through on the commitment in order to make someone else happy and reduce our own self-attachment.

▣▷ Over this past year, have you begun to develop a bodhisattva mentality? Do you see yourself as a person whom others can and should rely upon? Do you feel willing to shoulder the difficulties of others? If not, how can you move toward those things?

DAY 19

One of the most effective ways to train in a mind that benefits others is to rejoice in the happiness and success of others. When we rejoice in the good things that others have, we can be sure that we're avoiding a self-centered state of mind. The actions that we take based on that rejoicing are bound to be positive and in line with our positive motivation. One of the best things we can do to prepare for the moment of death is to rejoice genuinely, and rejoice often, in the happiness and success of others.

▣▷ Take a moment to notice the happiness of another, and allow yourself to rejoice in their success.

Day 20

▨▶ Today, notice how many times you express any one of the ten virtues of body, speech, and mind.

Reflect on yourself over the past year. Do you see a change in your behavior, such that you're expressing more positive conduct than before? Do you notice more positive thoughts and motivations in the mind?

Day 21

We can use the practice of tonglen in our reflections on the dying process. When we encounter someone who is ill or is facing tremendous physical suffering, we can use our inhalation to take their suffering upon ourselves. Along with our exhalation, we can send them feelings of comfort and well-being.

▨▶ Reflect on yourself over the past year. Has your fear of taking on the suffering of others decreased? Have you become more open to the pain and suffering that others experience, and more willing to share in their experiences? Have you become less fearful of doing a practice like tonglen?

Day 22

No matter what we give, we should give it without hesitation. If we're only capable of giving a penny right now with no feelings of greed or attachment, we should start by giving a penny. From there, we can work up to ten cents, a quarter, a dollar, five dollars, and so on. By starting out with something small and seemingly insignificant, we can begin to prepare for the moment of death, when we will have to leave all of our wealth and possessions behind.

✏️▷ What can you give now that you couldn't give a year ago? What are you still not able to give?

DAY 23

Listening to others is a form of generosity. We all know how it feels to talk to someone who only focuses the conversation on themselves and doesn't let us get a word in edgewise. Rather than getting frustrated that we weren't listened to fairly and equally, we can simply focus on the other person, doing our best to offer them relief and comfort.

✏️▷ Reflect on yourself now as compared to a year ago. Can you focus wholeheartedly on another person, offering them the gift of unselfish listening? Are you willing to be there for someone else without getting anything in return?

DAY 24

When we embody the meaning of our spiritual tradition, we naturally benefit those around us. When we express an attitude of love, kindness, or patience toward others, it's like rubbing salve on the wounds of those around us, who are stinging from all of the many sufferings and difficulties they face in life. When we take up virtuous conduct, we set an example of integrity and show a different way of living in the world.

✏️▷ Today, reflect on your very being as a vehicle to benefit others.

DAY 25

When we think of the possibility of dying confidently, we should realize that our own confident death would be inspirational to others. When we face death with assurance, we show others that it's possible to transcend the fear of death through spiritual practice. What greater generosity could we express than to help alleviate the fear others have of dying?

▆▆▷ Make an aspiration prayer that even the act of your death can be of benefit to those around you.

DAY 26

Generosity brings us willingness to change, to give up what we want for another, to be satisfied with what we have, to be flexible, to compromise, to cherish others more than ourselves. If we practice generosity with great diligence, the mind that wishes to benefit others will naturally arise. Opportunities to benefit others will not pass us by. And we will create our own chances to help and assist others through our generous spirit.

▆▆▷ What changes have you noticed in yourself with regard to generosity? Have you become more generous as a result of the past year's efforts?

DAY 27

▆▆▷ Today, right now, make an aspiration prayer for your own spiritual development, so that you may develop an unlimited potential to benefit others. Kindle a feeling of warmth in your heart, and send that wish to benefit all sentient beings out from your heart center. As you continue on with your day, try to keep that warm feeling in your heart, and engage in your ordinary activities as an expression of that heartfelt wish.

DAY 28

▭⇒ Have you continued to show up for scheduled practices and supported the activities of your spiritual community? Are there people in your spiritual community who could use your support? How can you be of service? Is there something you can do to assist your spiritual friend or make him or her more comfortable? Can you express your devotion through willingness to embody the meaning of his or her teachings?

DAY 29

Patience is our constant companion on the spiritual path. Armored with it, we'll continually give rise to the mind that aspires to benefit others. Patience is the source of endless good qualities. It is the wish-fulfilling gem that helps us to master perfect bodhichitta and the four immeasurable qualities.

▭⇒ Reflect on yourself over the past year. Have you become more patient and more willing to endure hardship for others? Has patience improved your connections with others?

DAY 30

▭⇒ Are you ready to die confidently? Have all of your preparations been made? Have you completed your Dharma Vision and Dharma Will, and assembled your Dharma Box, sufficiently to carry you through the next year? If any preparations are lacking, take time to complete them today.

Day 31

Take a few moments to rejoice in the effort you made during the past month. Dedicate any good that came from your contemplative practice for the benefit of all sentient beings.

Benediction

OVER THE PAST YEAR, you have taken yourself on a journey of self-discovery in relation to death, connecting deeply with others and the nature of samsara. Through your commitment to this contemplative program, your confidence in yourself and your practice has surely increased. We hope your commitment to daily practice won't stop here, but that this year's contemplation is just the beginning to your lifelong dedication to spiritual practice.

Index

About the Authors

 **ANYEN RINPOCHE** was born in Amdo, Tibet. His lineage can be traced back directly to the renowned Dzogchen master Patrul Rinpoche, author of *Words of My Perfect Teacher*. Anyen Rinpoche is a heart-son of Tsara Dharmakirti Rinpoche, a renowned master of the Longchen Nyingthig tradition as well as a *rime* (nonsectarian) master of Tibetan Buddhism. After remaining with his root lama for eighteen years, Anyen Rinpoche came to America, where he established the Orgyen Khamdroling Dharma Center in Denver, Colorado. Rinpoche's Dharma activity focuses on helping Buddhist practitioners prepare for the moment of death through the Dying with Confidence Program and the Phowa Foundation. He also teaches a traditional *shedra*, or intensive Vajrayana study, for Westerners at Orgyen Khamdroling.

 **ALLISON CHOYING ZANGMO** is a student of Anyen Rinpoche and his root master, Tsara Dharmakirti Rinpoche. She has been studying the Tibetan language and Buddhism under Anyen Rinpoche's personal guidance for the past sixteen years, and acts as his personal translator. She lives in Denver, Colorado.

Also Available by Anyen Rinpoche from Wisdom Publications

Dying with Confidence
A Tibetan Buddhist Guide to Preparing for Death
Anyen Rinpoche
Translated by Allison Choying Zangmo
Afterword by Tulku Thondup Rinpoche

"A powerful guidebook and a source of comfort at life's most crucial moment."—Tulku Thondup Rinpoche, author of *Boundless Healing*

Journey to Certainty
The Quintessence of the Dzogchen View:
An Exploration of Mipham's Beacon of Certainty
Anyen Rinpoche
Translated and edited by Allison Choying Zangmo

"Remarkably accessible, this book is essential reading for anyone attempting to understand or practice Dzogchen today."
—John Makransky, author of *Awakening Through Love*

Momentary Buddhahood
Mindfulness and the Vajrayana Path
Anyen Rinpoche
Translated by Allison Choying Zangmo
Foreword by Tulku Thondup Rinpoche

"An extraordinary book."—Deborah Schoeberlein David, author of *Mindful Teaching and Teaching Mindfulness*

Also Available from Wisdom Publications

The Grace in Aging
Awaken as You Grow Older
Kathleen Dowling Singh

"Don't grow old without it."—Rachel Naomi Remen, MD, author of *Kitchen Table Wisdom*

First Invite Love In
40 Time-Tested Tools for Creating a More Compassionate Life
Tana Pesso with His Holiness Penor Rinpoche
Foreword by His Holiness the Dalai Lama

"*First Invite Love In* is a clear, practical handbook that will genuinely help anyone who reads it and follows its exercises."—Sharon Salzberg, author of *Lovingkindness*

A Buddhist Grief Observed
Guy Newland

"A work of uncommon power, insight, and honesty."—Jay L. Garfield, author of *Engaging Buddhism*

Awake at the Bedside
Contemplative Teachings on Palliative and End-of-Life Care
Edited by Koshin Paley Ellison and Matt Weingast

"The more we care for the happiness of others, the greater is our own sense of well-being. Cultivating a close, warmhearted feeling for others automatically puts the mind at ease. It is the ultimate source of success in life. *Awake at the Bedside* supports this development of love and compassion."—His Holiness the Dalai Lama

About Wisdom Publications

Wisdom Publications is the leading publisher of classic and contemporary Buddhist books and practical works on mindfulness. To learn more about us or to explore our other books, please visit our website at wisdompubs.org or contact us at the address below.

Wisdom Publications
199 Elm Street
Somerville, MA 02144 USA

We are a 501(c)(3) organization, and donations in support of our mission are tax deductible.

Wisdom Publications is affiliated with the Foundation for the Preservation of the Mahayana Tradition (FPMT).

Thank you for buying this book!

Please visit wisdompubs.org/confidence
to get details on the free ebook awaiting you.